To Patti Ric...
Enjoy the Peninsula!
Barbara Dye

The Palos Verdes Peninsula -

A Place Set Apart

Many thanks to the following Docents at the
Point Vicente Interpretive Center
whose research papers were invaluable in
writing this book:

Lucy Ableser	Allen Hickman
Ethel Allen	Annette Howard
Bettina Arnold	Sue Kersey
Robert Baris	Jean Legge
Robert Benedict	Joan LeMere
Mary Bernatz	Connie Lufkin
Aileen Bevan	Bob Lusian
Mary-Jane Bloomingdale	Jack Macdonald
Lee Briggs	Carmen Marinella
Barbara Carpenter	Frances McCue
Earl Casler	Tom Mone
Julia Chichon	Marky Norwood
Whaja Cho	Alice Novick
Jan Coconis	Patricia Osterstock
Johanna Corbett	Ruth Pettengill
Patricia Daly	Shizue Prochaska
Norma Dodds	Emmy Reeves
Shel Downey	B. Arlyne Rehder
Joan Dox	Martin Reiter
Jo Doyle	Bill Ritchie
Eugene Feingold	Eva Risnel
Joseph Gorman	Nancy Rosenthal
Dorothy Gramlich	Vicki Schoenfeld
Sonia Handelsman	Jackie Scott
Donna Handley	Bea Semos
Emily Hansen	Ginny Shoren
Nan Harman	Jacqueline Theall
Bill Hearn	Robert Ulin
Gracie Henricks	Gwen Ward
Helen Hensinger	Anita Zinkin

A DRIVING TOUR

OF THE

PALOS VERDES PENINSULA

Second Edition

by

Barbara Dye

A DRIVING TOUR OF THE
PALOS VERDES PENINSULA,
Second Edition.

Library of Congress Catalog Card
Number 92-074729

ISBN 0-9634861-0-1

(previously ISBN 0-9620050-0-2) Published 1988 by the
Point Vicente Interpretive Center

Second Edition, 1992

Copyright 1992 by Barbara L.K. Dye

All rights reserved.
No part of this book may be reproduced in any form without the written consent of the author.

Published by Blickidy Press
7035 Hartcrest Drive
Rancho Palos Verdes, CA 90274

Table of Contents

Page

Introduction	1
How to Use This Book	4

1. Point Vicente Interpretive Center - museum exhibits ... coral trees, sea lavender and jasmine ... whale watching ... sea birds ... the lighthouse ... ghost stories. — 7

2. The Fishing Access Parking Lot - Santa Catalina Island ... fumeroles ... shipping ... goodbye Marineland ... Native American artifacts ... fruit and vegetable stands. — 14

3. Wayfarers Chapel - Chapel history ... Lloyd Wright, Helen Keller and Johnny Appleseed ... Swedenborgian religion ... shale, clay and lots of landslides ... preservation of open space ... the Gatehouse ... tumbleweed ... whaling days ... Portuguese Bend Club. — 22

4. Forrestal Drive - cliffs and crystals ... fossil fish ... sage and sagebrush ... coastal sage scrub habitat ... rattlesnakes. — 30

X. Short Cut - PV Drive East to Miraleste ... switchbacks ...cactus and grasses ...Marymount College ... radar towers — 37

5. White Point - lava flows, twisted rock and hot springs ... Japanese history on the Peninsula ... resorts and farms ... fear and friendship.   41

6. Point Fermin Park - Walker's Café ... yet another landslide ... The American Cetacean Society ... the Victorian lighthouse ... Dominguez vs. Sepulveda ... claims and counterclaims.   48

7. Angels Gate Park - Fort MacArthur ... great big guns ... military museum ... Korean Friendship Bell ... Marine Mammal Care and more.   54

8. Gaffey Overlook - harbor history ...Terminal Island ... Phineas T. Banning ... railroads and ripoffs ...the "Free Harbor controversy" ... secret tunnels ... Miraleste.   60

9. Georgeff Canyon - faults and folds ... old rocks and earthquakes ... small furry creatures ... water, water, where's the water?   68

10. General Store - ranchos and early ranching ... the Bixbys and the Phillips ... Rancho Elastico ... Rolling Hills ... rent a cow ... the world's happiest horse ... polo and fox hunting.   74

11. South Coast Botanic Garden - diatoms and daisies ... new flowers for our gardens ... great piles of trash ... methane power ... the Chadwick School ... the Art Center.   81

12. Del Cerro Park - view of the south coast ... the Vanderlips ... early estates ... Portuguese Point ... movie locations ... mustard and licorice ... radio ranch.   87

13. Indian Peak Overlook - lakes and valleys ... commercial development ... to mall or not to mall ... . Norris Theater ... the talking clock ... the Palos Verdes Peninsula Unified School District.   94

14. Silver Spur - the blimp in the sky ... city view ... the Palos Verdes Project ... early visions ... con men and dreamers ... The Homes Association ... landscaping ... the Golf Club.   100

15. La Venta Inn - early hospitality ... sell that lot ... celebrity visitors ... notable homes ... Farnham Martin's Park and Fountain ... Malaga Cove Library.   106

16. Malaga Cove Plaza - the community gets organized ... the Gardner Building ... Casa del Portal ... King Neptune in marble ... eucalyptus trees ... Olmstead house ... PV slides into the ocean ... Malaga Cove School.   112

17. Malaga Cove - Native American village site ... RAT Beach ... Roessler Pool ... Haggerty house ... all nudes is good nudes ... the Neighborhood Church.   119

18. Bluff Cove - little Waikiki ... the mystery of the Chinese anchors ... a grandiose yacht club ... the Douglas Cut ... dynamite and roadbuilding ... the Project has trouble ... the Parklands Controversy... incorporation.   125

19. Lunada Bay - guns on the coastline ... the wreck of the Dominator ... kelp comes back ... tide pool dwellers.   131

20. Lunada Bay Patio Building - Spanish plans ... La Fuente de los Niños ... coastal development ... terraces and time ... the infamous blue butterfly ... A Place Set Apart.   138

Handicapped Access   144

Bibliography   146

Index   149

The Point Vicente Interpretive Center overlooks the Pacific Ocean in Rancho Palos Verdes.

Introduction

It's funny how fate leads us down unexpected pathways. The story of how this book came to be written is very much a story of choices, and trips down pathways full of surprises.

When my husband was transferred from Princeton to Los Angeles in 1986, our Realtor sent us a book describing all the communities in the region. We read the book and both agreed that Palos Verdes was the place we wanted to live, because of the excellent school system and the trails and open spaces. We flew out (with our then three-week old daughter, Victoria), spent a hectic week house hunting, found and bought a house.

Several months later the whole family moved to Rancho Palos Verdes. Once our two older daughters, Katie and Nora, had started school, I looked around for some volunteer work to do. I took the girls to the Point Vicente Interpretive Center one day and saw that they had a new Docent training class starting.

"Do you have anything I can do with my baby?" I asked. "Sure," they answered. "You can do everything with your baby." And thus a wonderful experience began.

Led by a knowledgeable, cheerful and interesting woman named Diana McIntyre, the Docent class learned about whales, lighthouses, sea birds, history and geography and visited every museum in the area. (Victoria, who by this time was five months old, listened but didn't contribute much.) One of the most enjoyable of the classes was the very first one, where Diana led the group on a driving tour much like this one. I recommend Docent training for anyone with time and an interest in the natural world.

In order to graduate from the Docent class, each trainee is expected to research and present a 15-minute paper on a subject related to the Peninsula. I asked if I could do something a bit more ambitious - a pamphlet describing a driving tour of the Peninsula. In a great leap of faith, they agreed. It turned out not to be that simple. As I researched the subject there was too much fascinating information for just a pamphlet, and the pamphlet turned into a book. All the papers by previous classes of Docents were on file at the Interpretive Center and they were full of material and saved me hours of research time.

Many people helped with the book. I took Martin Reiter's class on *The Geology of the Palos Verdes Peninsula* and found his book extremely helpful. Carmen Marinella, a local historian and Docent at the Interpretive Center, proofed the manuscript for historical accuracy and allowed me to use his bibliography. Mary Thomas, Director of the Recreation and Parks Department for the City of Rancho Palos Verdes (which includes the Interpretive Center), edited, advised, assisted and supported the project. Many others helped, including Nancy Pierce, Director of the Interpretive Center, and Diana McIntyre, without whose enthusiastic support, help and information the book would not exist.

The book was quite a success, and 4,000 copies of the first edition sold out in just a few years. People seemed to find the level of detail about right - a little marine science mixed with a little geology and a pinch of botany all stirred together in a history base.

People began to ask when I would be doing a second edition, but I had become too involved in community work to find time for my own enterprises. Finally, I heard that the library made people surrender their driver's licenses for the right to look at the book and I decided that the time had come.

This version of the book is very much the same as the first edition. Having only lived here a year when I wrote it, I made a few mistakes but since it really is just a little bit of

*The relief map at the Interpretive Center
is a good place to start your tour.*

this and that, the facts remain the same. I've added new material about local habitat and how important it is to preserve some of the open space on the Peninsula so that future generations can enjoy the sight of a mariposa lily or the call of a gnatcatcher. As I've come across interesting stories I've saved them for the book. Development has made significant alterations to the natural features and I've tried to point out what has changed in five years and what the plans are for the future of this Peninsula.

A number of people have added to my knowledge of the Peninsula. Don Gales, whose wonderful book *Wildflowers, Weeds, Wildlife, & Weather of P.V.* should be on everyone's book shelf, took time to share his abundant awareness of Peninsula natural history with me. Angelika Brinkmann-Busi, President of the local Native Plant Society, taught me about the local flora and brought to life the importance of what we have worth preserving here. Jess Morton, Mike Kilroy, Carmen Marinella (again!), Bill Ritchie, Emmy Reeves, Mary-Jane Bloomingdale, Marky Norwood, Jill Link, Elise Gorman, and Alan Franz all taught me something new about our Peninsula.

I must express my appreciation to my family, who cope with a busy Mother with too much to do. I also want to thank others who've provided help and support: Terri Ahn, Sylvia Alvarado, Consuelo Franco, Sheri Hastings and Ruth Macfarlane. Dave at DSK Photo did a wonderful job of developing and printing the photographs.

At the Interpretive Center, the Peninsula is referred to as "A Place Set Apart". As I've learned more about the area I understand what is meant by that phrase. This is one of the most scenic and historic parts of southern California. Its five communities - Palos Verdes Estates, Rolling Hills, Rolling Hills Estates, Rancho Palos Verdes and San Pedro - occupy land that juts out into the ocean from the Los Angeles basin. Ocean breezes blow across its hillsides, bringing clean but sometimes foggy air. The geologic fault that separates the Peninsula from the rest of Los Angeles, leaves it higher, dryer, and psychologically isolated from the city below.

The more I learn the more I see that the history of the Peninsula is largely separate from that of the surrounding area, though the two have intertwined and interacted through the centuries. The unique climate also brings its own special complement of birds, animals and plants characteristic of the cliffs and canyons of the Peninsula.

Whether you are visiting the Peninsula from far away, looking for a pleasant day-trip, considering a move here, or trying to learn about your own community, this driving tour will give you some background on this "Place Set Apart."

- Barbara Dye

How to Use This Book

The Driving Tour is a circle approximately 38 miles long around the Palos Verdes Peninsula. It is divided into 20 stops. Each Stop, or Chapter, discusses the history of that spot and includes additional information on related subjects. Then the guide will take you to the next stop, indicating points of interest along the route. It is recommended that you read the whole chapter before driving so you aren't trying to read and travel at the same time.

Cumulative mileage for each chapter is indicated in the right-hand margin, and mileage on the road is specified in the text. On the back cover you will find a map showing the stops and the route of the tour. The tour is designed to begin and end at the Point Vicente Interpretive Center, but any chapter can be done on its own.

Each paragraph has a word highlighted in boldface within it. This word summarizes the content of the paragraph and will help you pick and choose the specific information that interests you in the tour. For example, in the first chapter you can skip the paragraphs in which pelicans and cormorants are highlighted if birds are not your thing.

All of the stops involve parking and getting out of your car. Eleven of the stops are simply a matter of admiring the view. Seven of the stops require a very short stroll. Two have optional walks, one a half-mile round trip, one just over a mile. There are six opportunities to take trails down to the ocean, though the tour doesn't require any descent of the cliffs.

Restrooms are available at the Interpretive Center, Fishing Access, Wayfarers Chapel, Point Fermin Park, Angels Gate Park, General Store, Botanic Garden and Malaga Cove Library.

An outdoor cafe at Lunada Bay Plaza

There are restaurants at Point Fermin Park, the General Store, and Lunada Bay Plaza, as well as in San Pedro, Miraleste Plaza, Peninsula Center, Lunada Bay Plaza and Golden Cove Plaza.

The Point Vicente Interpretive Center has an admission fee for the museum but there is plenty to see from the park around the building. Docents are on hand to provide a guided tour of the museum, which will greatly enhance your understanding of the Peninsula and its resources.

The Botanic Garden also has an admission fee, but entrance to the gift shop is free.

Start your driving tour of the Palos Verdes Peninsula in the parking lot of the Point Vicente Interpretive Center, at 31501 Palos Verdes Drive West. The Center is south of the junction of Hawthorne Boulevard and Palos Verdes Drive West, adjacent to the Point Vicente Lighthouse.

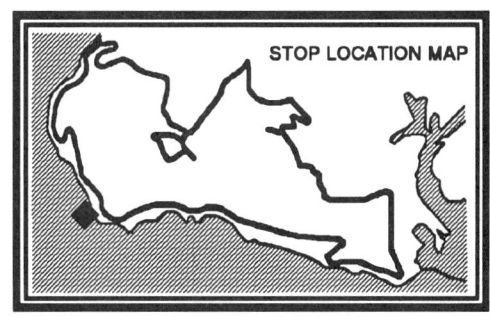

◆**Stop 1.**

Point Vicente Interpretive Center

The square, pop-top building perched on the cliff top ahead of you is a small museum dedicated to the Palos Verdes Peninsula, "a place set apart." The **28-acre park** which surrounds it has a picnic area, fields of cultivated garbanzo beans and baby's breath, and natural areas where native plants are encouraged to grow.

The museum, called the **Point Vicente Interpretive Center**, was built by the city of Rancho Palos Verdes at a cost of $1.3 million, and opened in 1984. It is small but rich in treasures illuminating the history and natural features of the Peninsula. Notable are the historic exhibits - including a full-scale replica of the doorway of the historic Banning House in Wilmington, photographs of early residents, relics of the Native Americans who once lived here, and a model of Cabrillo's ship.

Children particularly enjoy the whale exhibits, where they can listen to recorded whale songs and admire the 15'-long model of a gray whale (which was made in Iowa, of all places, and completed while on display at the State Fair). Also of interest is the relief map of the Peninsula, a good place to **orient yourself** before starting the driving tour.

Visitors will also want to look at the exhibits on the landslide, local archeology, and animal life, before climbing to admire the view from the tower windows. **Admission** to the Museum is $2.00 for adults; $1.00 for children, handicapped individuals, and senior citizens. The Center opens at noon every day except Tuesday, and is open until 5 p.m. in winter, 7 p.m. in summer. The restroom entrances are on the outside of the building.

The large smooth-trunked tree to the left of the entrance of the museum is a Natal **coral tree**, an import from South Africa that bears bright orange flowers in the spring. The plants with wide, dusty green leaves and tall purple flowers that grow all around the Center are **sea lavender**, also known as statice, a perennial that in its wild form (called limonium) is native to California. The sweet smell that fills the air in springtime is from the white-flowered **honeysuckle** vines that sprawl beside the center and from the **jasmine** plants, with their glossy dark green leaves and white flowers.

From the pathways along the clifftop and the terrace at the back of the museum you have a **splendid view** of the ocean from Malibu to the island of Catalina and a direct view straight down to the surf pounding on the base of the cliffs.

Santa Barbara Island, a small, two-humped bump, can be seen just on the horizon on clear days. The plants on this side of the Center are all California natives, planted and tended by the California Native Plant Society.

During the spring months you may see some black birds that look like question marks nesting in the cliffs. These are **cormorants**, fish-eaters that swim underwater to catch their prey. Their nests of seaweed hold from three to six chalky, bluish eggs. In ancient times the Chinese placed a ring around a cormorant's neck, let it fish, pulled the bird in with a rope, and then removed the fish that the bird had been unable to swallow.

Brown **pelicans** also cruise along the wave tops below the Peninsula. The birds are only brown for their first few years, changing to gray at maturity, with a black belly and white head and neck. With a wing span of up to eight feet, they often fly in long lines or V's of birds, their slow, heavy wing beats alternating with periods where they seem to sail through the air.

Pelicans **nest** in **colonies** on the islands off the coast. The males choose the nest site on a cliff top or ledge and then attract a female with head bobbing and weaving. They then bring sticks so the females can build nests. The male and female take turns covering the eggs with their feet until the chicks hatch.

Pelicans have binocular vision and can spot fish swimming below the surface. Once the prey is spotted, the pelican folds its wings halfway and dives into the water, scooping up the **fish** in its bill. Once it surfaces, the bird holds its bill downward to let the water drain out before swallowing the fish whole.

Pelicans can live up to 35 years, but as recently as 1969 were an **endangered species**. At that time the major breeding colony on Anacapa Island went from 3000 nesting pairs to 250 and the eggshells became so thin that they shattered when the parents tried to incubate them. The problem was traced to a DDT processing plant that was dumping its waste material into the Los Angeles sewer system, which in turn dumped it into the harbor. In 1972 the DDT dumping was stopped and today the Anacapa colony is up to almost full strength. Deposits of DDT still remain off the Peninsula's coastline, however, buried by sediments and only affecting bottom-feeding organisms.

A number of different types of **gulls** can be seen on the southern California coastline. Identification can be tricky since they change their appearance as they mature and with the season of the year. A good guidebook with pictures is really the only way to be sure, but here are some tips to help you identify the most common types here.

> The **Ring bill gull** has a white body, grayish back and wings, yellowish-green legs, and a black ring around tip of its yellow bill.
>
> The **Western gull** is larger in size, with a very dark gray back and wings, a yellow bill with a red spot near its lower tip, and pink legs.
>
> The **Heerman's gull** has a dark gray body with a black tail, a white head, a red bill, and black feet.

Among the **nearly 400** other birds seen on the Peninsula are great horned owls (with their characteristic deep hoo-hooo-hooo), hummingbirds (including the rare Allen's hummingbird), red-tailed hawks, road runners, mourning doves and quail.

In the winter you will see the official "**whale watch**" crew (affiliated with the American Cetacean Society and the Cabrillo Marine Museum) counting the whales that swim by on their yearly migration. The watchers would prefer not to be asked a lot of questions, but by observing where they are looking you'll improve your chances of spotting a passing whale. In the spring the watchers move to the other side of the point where they can see the whales coming for a longer distance.

Gray whales pass the summer in the shallow waters of the

Bering and Chukchi Seas where they feed on small bottom dwellers that they strain through the filter plates, called baleen, in their upper jaws. In the fall the whales head south, with the pregnant females (about half are pregnant each year) leading the way. Traveling in small groups called pods the whales swim from 90 to 100 miles per day, heading for the lagoons of Baja California where many of the babies will be born.

As the **whales** swim by the coast they surface to breathe and their spouts can be **spotted** fairly easily by the patient observer. Look for a small white cloud of mist, somewhat heart-shaped. The whales blow, descend for about a minute, blow again, descend for another minute, blow again and then do a deep dive, staying down for from four to seven minutes.

A whale blows off Pt. Vicente

Before the last dive whales often lift their tail flukes out of the water. Sometimes they also lift their heads out of the water to look around (called **spyhopping**) or leap almost entirely out of the water and crash back down (called **breaching**). Nobody knows why they breach, but some speculate that it just may be fun!

The Interpretive Center Docents keep a **running talley** of the number of whales that have passed by each season and each day on a blackboard. In recent years the number has decreased and some speculate that the whales are annoyed by the admittedly not-always-polite whale watch boats and are choosing to swim on the other side of Catalina.

On the tip of the point near the Interpretive Center you will see the **Point Vicente Lighthouse**, built in 1926 by the U.S. Lighthouse Service. The point was named by George Vancouver for Padre Vincente Santa Maria, who had been very hospitable to him when he visited Mission Buenaventura. So many ships were wrecked on the rocks below this point that ships' captains joined together and petitioned the government to help them avoid the danger.

The lighthouse is 67 feet high and stands on a cliff 130 feet high, placing it 197 feet above the ocean and making it visible from 20 miles away. The Fresnel **lens** is French, has 52 hand-ground glass lenses, and was made in Paris in 1888. It saw 40 years of service in Alaska before being transferred here. The light, controlled remotely from the U.S. Coast Guard station in L.A. Harbor, flashes every 20 seconds and is supplemented by an electronically-operated foghorn in the little box on the edge of the cliff. Human beings have thus been completely replaced by machines in the modern lighthouse business.

There are several **legends** attached to the lighthouse, mostly revolving around the misty figure of a woman who circles the upper walkway or runs to the cliff edge. One story tells of a lost lighthouse keeper who went off to aid a ship on a stormy night, leaving a distraught wife or daughter to keep vigil. Another tells of a woman who threw herself off the cliff to join her sailor lover lost at sea. Realists suggest that the ghosts appeared at the time the landward windows of the lighthouse were covered with paint, but many prefer the touch of romance and mystery provided by the lady of the lighthouse.

The buildings on the site provide **housing** for Coast Guard officers who work elsewhere. The federal government has expressed its intention to build addition units of homes with an incredible view. In the original plan for the development of the Peninsula, the hillside behind the museum, on the other side of Palos Verdes Drive, was to have been the site for an Italian **artisans village** where craftsmen would live, work, and sell their wares. Those plans, unfortunately, were abandoned during the Depression.

During the World Wars, the hillside was one site for **coastal artillery**, part of the harbor defenses of Los Angeles. In World War II this was Battery Harry C. Barnes, named for a Coast Artillery Officer and West Point graduate who was stationed at Fort MacArthur in the 1930's. It held a medium range coastal defense gun normally used against small cruisers and light craft.

Manholes and air vents (you can see at least one small cement construction) on the hillsides mark **underground tunnels** where there were lookout posts and sites for gun emplacements. Soldiers were camped at Pt. Vicente during World War II to man the guns and the observation posts.

Further back are the silos for the **Nike missiles** that were installed in 1954 and deactivated in the early 1970's. The facility is four-stories deep, and was ringed by berms and barbed wire. The missiles were stored horizontally, rolled to the launch platform, and then lifted into a near-vertical position for launch. They were intended to destroy fleets of enemy bombers that might approach the Peninsula. The buildings that were part of the missile base now serve as Rancho Palos Verdes City Hall.

From the Interpretive Center turn right onto Palos Verdes Drive West and drive .5 mile to the Fishing Access site on the right-hand side of the road. Park in the lot.

◆ **Stop 2.**

Fishing Access Parking Lot

From the parking lot you have a **view** of the former site of Marineland on Long Point and the island of Catalina. Public restrooms are located at the western end of the parking lot, and a very steep trail down to the ocean begins just past them. The access was constructed and is maintained by the Los Angeles County Department of Beaches.

Santa **Catalina** Island is 21 miles long and 2,125 feet at its highest point. Visible on clear days, it rises out of the ocean like a magical land due south of the Peninsula. Many evidences of Native American history have been found on

Catalina, and it was evidently the source of an easily-carved mineral called steatite (or soapstone) that was traded as far north as the Santa Barbara area.

Juan Rodriguez **Cabrillo** visited Catalina in 1542 on his voyage of discovery, naming the island for Saint Catherine, whose saint's day it was. In 1846 Pio Pico, the Mexican Governor of Alta California, gave title to the island to Thomas Robbins in exchange for a silver saddle, a canny trade if there ever was one.

Later the island belonged to the Banning family, who began trying in 1887 to develop a **tourist industry**, providing tent spaces instead of hotel rooms. Unfortunately, the lure of canvas walls and wooden floors was not enough to inspire city dwellers to make the difficult ocean crossing from L.A. and the venture was never very successful.

In 1919 most of the island was purchased by William **Wrigley**, of chewing gum fame, who was determined to preserve much of the island in its natural state. He built a summer home, an aviary and a botanic garden, and made the island the spring training camp for the Chicago Cubs baseball team. In 1975 the Wrigleys donated 86% of the island to the **Santa Catalina Conservancy**, which maintains it as a unique wildlife refuge, rare native plant habitat, and open space preserve. Notable are the herds of bison, descendants of a group brought for the filming of a movie called The *Vanishing American* in 1924.

Tourists can travel to Avalon (Catalina's only city) and to Two Harbors (on the Isthmus) from **ferries** from San Pedro or Long Beach. The trip takes two to three hours.

You may well see ships traveling past you, to and from Los Angeles harbor to the east around the Peninsula. There are mile-wide **Shipping zones** off the coast here - the northbound lane is closest, separated by a mile from the southbound lane.

If you take the **trail** down to the water you will find fascinating tide pools full of marine life. Toward Long Point you may smell sulphur, coming up mixed with other gasses from deep within the earth through passages called fumeroles. Be careful when scrambling around on the rocks: sudden waves have been known to sweep people out to sea. Cracks in the rocks have been filled with small dolomite crystals, cream colored with a triangular cross section.

Sea Lions on a buoy off the Redondo Pier

A number of different **sea mammals** live off the coast in this area, and you may see some basking in the sun on the rocks below Long Point. The most common is the California sea lion, the relatively intelligent animal used in oceanarium and circus shows. Male **California sea lions** grow up to 8 feet long and may weigh as much as 800 pounds. The females are smaller, growing up to 6 feet long and weighing up to 250 pounds. Each spring the sea lions congregate on island "rookeries" where each male has a harem of 10 to 20 females, each one of whom will give birth to a single pup. Sea lions differ from seals in having ears outside their bodies and hind flippers that can bend under their bodies.

The **elephant seal** is the largest seal found in the northern hemisphere, with 20'-long males weighing up to 3 tons. Their overdeveloped noses actually work as resonating chambers, making their mating roars loud and intimidating to rivals. They breed, have babies, and go through a molting period on islands off the coast. It is mainly single, subadult or older males who don't fit into the social hierarchy on the islands who are occasionally seen in coastal coves.

Sea otters are the smallest marine mammals, with 5-foot-long males weighing up to 100 pounds and 4-foot females up to 60 pounds. They are playful by nature and can be seen joining their babies in a round of tag or other games offshore. They have an extremely high metabolism and must consume as much as 25% of their body weight in shellfish, crabs, sea urchins and assorted other sea creatures each day. After gathering food and storing it in pouches on their chests, the otters bring up stones and crack the shells on their chests to get at the meat. Although they are rare around the Peninsula, a few have been seen in recent years.

All of these sea mammals were close to **extinction** at the end of the 19th century. The sea otter's fur is thick, soft and waterproof, and was in such great demand that more than 100,000 were killed in 30 years. In 1911 the Fur Seal Treaty protected them on the high seas, and in 1913 Alaska and California gave them full protection. Today commercial fishermen complain that expanding populations of otters compete unfairly with them for fish, a controversy that has yet to be resolved. Elephant seals were an excellent source of lamp oil, so they were extensively hunted. By 1892 only about 100 were left, but fortunately they were **protected** by the Mexican government in 1911 and began to reestablish their colonies. Sea lions were hunted after other sources of oil and fur were exhausted and they too were reduced to small colonies on the islands. They now have returned but are also in conflict with fishermen who claim that they steal from their fishing nets.

MILEAGE	
0	*Turn right on Palos Verdes Drive South, and continue 1.6 miles to the Wayfarers Chapel.*
.5	On your right you will pass the abandoned gates of **Marineland**. Founded in 1952 by a New York stockbroker as the second aquatic park in the country, Oceanarium, Inc. (as it then was called), opened in

1954. Its first star was a trained pilot whale named Bubbles who lured more than a million visitors to the park in 1957. Hollywood welcomed the new enterprise, using it as a backdrop for movies and shows, the most famous of which was *Sea Hunt*. The park, renamed Marineland, was also known for its care of sick and injured sea animals.

After Sea World opened in San Diego, attendance dropped off at the park. It was sold in 1970, leased in 1973 and sold again in 1977 and 1981. The new owners all tried to bring in more revenues but were largely **unsuccessful**. *Baja Reef*, a swim-through aquarium, and *Project Discovery*, a program to help teachers present marine life to their classes, were both innovative introductions to the facility. The biggest stars, however, were **Orky and Corky**, trained killer whales.

In December of 1986 **Marineland** was **sold** to Harcourt, Brace & Jovanovich, Publishers, owner of Sea World. In spite of protests from local citizens, they removed all the animals and announced that the land was for sale.

The 108-acre park was finally sold to a developer, who now refers to the area as "Long Point". The land is zoned commercial-recreational, and the owner has received permission to build a 450-room **luxury hotel**, with a 9-hole golf course and a conference center. The project was approved by the City and the Coastal Commission, but as of 1992 was on hold for financial reasons. Public access to the coastline is still permitted in certain areas during daylight.

The **animal care center**, which rescued and nursed sick and hurt animals for the entire L. A County coastline, has now been moved to Fort MacArthur in San Pedro. Harcourt, Brace, & Jovanovich donated $3 million to support construction of the facility, which will be run in cooperation with the L.A. Unified School District.

MILEAGE
.5

Fishing Access

MILEAGE	
.7	To the east of Marineland at the top of the cliff Native American **artifacts** have been found, including numerous flakes of chert, a waxy-looking, very hard, brittle material found in some sedimentary rocks and used for arrowheads.
.9	The intensive **development** east of Long Point was largely completed under approvals given by the County before the City of Rancho Palos Verdes was incorporated.
1.4	Past the former Marineland parking lot you will see the **flower stand** of Mae Ishibashi, and outside the Abalone Cove parking lot the flower and vegetable stand of Annie and James Ishibashi. All of their produce and flowers are grown on the Peninsula.
1.4	Entrance to the **Abalone Cove Shoreline Park** parking lot is $5, and it is the only legal place to park for the next two miles. There's a steep but fairly easy trail to the shore area. The area belongs to the City's Redevelopment Agency which has the responsibility for slowing land movement in the area. Docent tours of the slopes and tidepools can be arranged by calling the Interpretive Center. Don't go out on the rocks to the east - big waves can come up suddenly. During excavation for the beach club a number of arrowheads and soapstone amulets were found. **Archeological investigations** indicated that there had been a kitchen midden (or food preparation site) and burial ground in the area. Fourteen graves were uncovered, with artifacts including a decorated soapstone pipe and a spectacular bead necklace made from clam and abalone shells (now in a private collection). Those involved in the dig speculated that this was a Native American fishing site, returned to periodically from villages near better water sources further east (probably near Machado Lake). Fish was probably smoked to be taken back to the village.
1.6	*Turn left into the Wayfarers Chapel parking lot.*

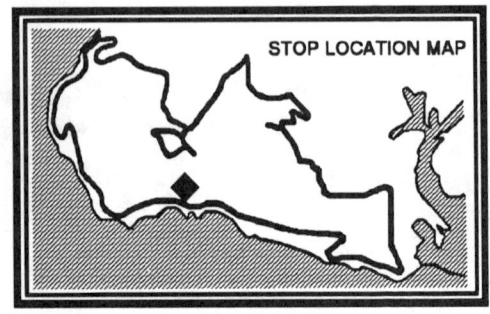

◆Stop 3.

THE WAYFARERS CHAPEL

One of the highlights of any tour of the Palos Verdes Peninsula is a visit to this lovely **glass chapel** overlooking the ocean. Admission to the chapel and grounds is free, though donations are gratefully accepted. There are public restrooms at the far end of the Visitor Center, though they may be closed at some point due to landslide damage.

The Wayfarers Chapel was the **dream** of Elizabeth Schellenberg, a member of the Swedenborgian Church in the late 1920's. Her friend Narcissa Cox Vanderlip, a member of the church and of the family that was beginning to develop the Peninsula, donated the land, and they asked a young architect named Ralph Jester for a design.

The Depression and World War II delayed the project, but after the war Mr. Jester asked his friend **Lloyd Wright** (son of Frank Lloyd Wright) to design the church. Since the Swedenborgian Church believes in the "essential harmony of creation, showing the interrelationship between the physical and the spiritual dimensions of reality," he envisioned a chapel that would blend nature and spirit. Inspired by a visit to the California redwoods, he designed a soaring building of glass, redwood and stone.

The church was dedicated in 1951, the tower added in 1954, and the Visitor Center built in 1958. Many local residents have been baptized and married in the chapel, which is open to people of all faiths and denominations. Several soap opera and movie weddings have even been filmed at the chapel. **Services** are conducted every Sunday at 11 a.m., and special Christmas and Easter services are a Peninsula tradition. There is no formal congregation, and all are welcome.

The **Swedenborgian** brand of **Christianity** was founded by Emmanuel Swedenborg, who was born in Sweden in 1688. He was a mathematician and scientist of broad interests and great intellect. He wrote more than 30 religious books, examining the relationship between body and soul. Displays outside provide information about the religion and two of its most famous members - Helen Keller and Johnny Appleseed.

The 3.5-acre grounds contain formal **gardens**, lawns and a hillside stream. Although the chapel itself is on firm land, the Visitor Center is on the Abalone Cove landslide and its interior has been closed to vistors.

Before you leave the Wayfarers Chapel it would be a good idea to **read the rest of this section**. There is a lot of material on the slide and the history of the area that will be difficult to read on the bumpy road ahead.

MILEAGE

Return to Palos Verdes Drive South. Turn left. 0

If you look quickly up to the left you can see the precarious position of the Visitor Center. Attempts have been made to shore it

.1

MILEAGE up with wooden beams, but it is clear that the **landslides** have left it with unstable foundations. The Chapel itself is fortunately on stable rock and is not in danger.

The area ahead and the hillside above it were the part of the Peninsula chosen by Frank **Vanderlip** for his own **estate** in the early 1920's. In order to select the best location, he had a climatologist come to live on the Peninsula. As you will see, he would have done much better to have sent a geologist.

You are about to drive across **the famous Palos Verdes landslides**, which have been called "the largest active landslides in the country." You will notice dips and cracks across the road surface, which must be repaved to keep the road open. The City of Rancho Palos Verdes was at one time spending as much as $300,000 per year to maintain less than a mile of road. You will also notice sewer and water pipes above the ground, with expansion joints to keep the pipes from breaking.

There are a number of different landslides in this area. None of them are new; **ancient landslides** were marked on early maps of the area. Today geological investigations of the Peninsula have identified those areas subject to slide activity, and have found that most of the Peninsula is steady as a rock.

.2 You will first cross the **Abalone Cove landslide**, between the Wayfarers Chapel and Portuguese Point. This became reactivated in 1974, due most likely to seasons of heavy rains. Dewatering wells that remove water and pipe it to the ocean have largely stopped this slide. Plans for stabilizing it include the possibility of constructing a toe berm, a large cement wall, at the foot of the slide in Abalone Cove, to prevent the ocean from washing away the landslide sediments.

	MILEAGE
Notice the gate house, sometimes called **Portuguese Bend Lodge**, on the right. It was built in the late 20's by Edward Harden, who was married to Frank Vanderlip's sister Ruth. He wanted an estate to rival that of William Randolph Hearst but it was never completed. The Historical Society placed a plaque on it in 1990, and at one time Neil Armstrong, the Astronaut, lived there.	.3
Just after the Lodge is **Portuguese Point**, with trails out to its tip, followed by Sacred Cove and Inspiration Point.	.3
On your left, inside the second gate to the Portuguese Bend residential area, is **Villa Francesca**, named for Harry Benedict's wife, Frances Homberg Benedict. It is also commemmorated by a plaque from the Historical Society.	.4

The **geology** of the Palos Verdes Peninsula is not particularly complex. The oldest rocks are a greenish-brown, metamorphic formation called the "Catalina Schist". This is of Mesozoic Age (dinosaur time, 80-225 million years ago), and can only be seen in a few spots on the Peninsula. After this schist was deposited and then melted and altered, millions of years passed. During the Miocene Epoch (25-35 million years ago) the schist was submerged, and muddy swamps and beaches alternated, depositing a shale and mudstone formation known as "Altamira Shale".

As the shale was being deposited there were also **volcanos** to the south which had at least one eruption of volcanic ash. It is this ash that is largely causing the landslide problem, since it has been altered to a clay which becomes very slippery when it gets wet.

The second, and larger, landslide you will cross is called the **Portuguese Bend landslide**. It covers about 300 acres and extends inland almost a mile.   1.0

In the early 1950's the Los Angeles County Road Department tried to complete Crenshaw Boulevard, planning to bring it down the southern hillside to Palos Verdes Drive. They excavated the roadbed and dumped more than 200,000 tons of material on top of the slide. On August 29, **1956, land movement** caused a water main to break, which added large amounts of water to the soil. Within a few days houses started to shift and break up and residents had to evacuate. More than 100 homes were completely destroyed, along with the Portuguese Bend Clubhouse and Pier. Homeowners sued L.A. County and others and were awarded more than $10 million.

In 1984 the City set up a **Redevelopment Agency** (RDA) to finance landslide abatement efforts. The RDA allows the City to keep a larger share of the property taxes paid by homes and landowners within the district, with the money used for abatement work. The RDA is also eligible to receive other grants from the state and federal governments for its abatement projects.

In 1986 a $2 million state grant was given to the RDA to **combat the slide.** Some 600,000 cubic yards of dirt were moved from the top of the slide to a position lower down where it inhibited further movement, and both sections were seeded with grass. Water collection basins were put in the canyons, with surface culverts to carry the water to the ocean. Movement slowed from 1.25 inches per day to less than 12 inches per year.

Experts expect the slide to slow further but accurate prediction is difficult. **Additional steps** that may be taken **to stop the slide** include drilling further wells to remove more deep water, grading to remove cracks and fissures, and building a barrier at the base of the slide to prevent erosion at the toe and to keep sea water from entering the slide. The City has placed temporary barriers, called "gabions" at the high tide mark at the base of this slide. They are cages of wire, filled with rocks.

The slide has continued at a somewhat slower rate ever since. Most **homes** were **abandoned** and razed, but a few

Rare Mariposa lilies bloom below an outcropping of pillow lava.

MILEAGE
1

determined families supported their homes on steel beams so that the building would at least slide in one piece. You will see two such houses on the left.

MILEAGE 1.5 As you cross the slide you can look down to the right at **Portuguese Bend Beach**. Notice how silty the water is from material brought down by the landslide, and notice how it is cleaner at the west end where the gabions prevent the sediments from entering the ocean. You can also see the beds of kelp, a brown seaweed, growing offshore where the water is cleaner.

Because of concern about its stability, a 1000-acre horseshoe of land on the north side of Palos Verdes Drive South has been placed in a development moratorium by the City. The **Palos Verdes Peninsula Land Conservancy,** a nonprofit, nonpolitical group organized by local residents, has proposed making this area a nature preserve, and is working with residents and state and local governments to accomplish this goal. The developers who own the land are attempting to demonstrate that parts of it are stable enough for possible homes and a golf course. (For information on the Palos Verdes Peninsula Land Conservancy, call 373-0202.)

Appropriately enough, the round green or brown (depending on the season) bushes that line the road through the slide are **tumbleweed**. The plant is really a newcomer called *Russian thistle* that arrived in Minnesota with Russian winter wheat about a hundred years ago. It rolled and seeded itself in a westerly direction, arriving here earlier in this century. Cowboy movies supposedly set in the 1800's that show tumbling tumbleweeds are therefore out of step with time.

During the 1870's a group of Portuguese **whalers** brought a prefabricated cabin around the Horn and settled in the cove to hunt for whales. Later in the 19th century whaling companies like the Portuguese Company, the Portuguese-American Company, and the John Brown Whaling Company, used the cove as a whaling station. Lookouts stood on the point and signalled down to whalers on the beach, who would then put to sea in their small MILEAGE boats, kill the whale, and tow the whale carcass back to the beach. There, an apparatus with ropes and pulleys would help them roll the whale so the fat could be stripped off. The blubber, meat, and bone were then processed into oil in two huge copper kettles hung over a sort of furnace. Between 1874 and 1877, 2,166 barrels of oil were produced, but then the station was abandoned for lack of fuel for the furnaces.

Around 1900 a Swedish fisherman named Charles Lundquist moved into the cabin and, using what may have been the whalers' iron pots, provided **fish dinners** for yachtsmen and visitors at a cost of 25 cents. Charlie's cabin, furniture, and pots remained until World War II, when they were scrapped for salvage.

Shortly after the end of the slide you will see on the right the parking lot and gated entrance to the **Portuguese Bend Club.** This is a private beach club with a waiting list for new members. It was founded in the late 1940's and grew quickly. By 1950 the club had a 50-foot pool and a 485-foot pier. Performing seals were featured at the pool for a Labor Day party, along with a complete luau done by a chef brought in from Hawaii. Two years later some 30,000 people gathered on the slopes to see a fireworks display on Independence Day. When the landslide began many houses at the beach club were affected, and the pier and pool were destroyed.

1.6

Continue on Palos Verdes Drive. Turn left onto Forrestal Drive.

2.2

Continue to the end. You can park at the Ladera Linda Community Center or on the side of the road near the top. Please don't block the gate, however; it provides access to the soccer field.

2.5

Wayfarers Chapel 🌿 Page 29

◆**Stop 4.**

Forrestal Drive

You are at the base of **Klondike Canyon**, named hopefully after the Alaska gold fields when gold (though it turned out to be pyrite, or fool's gold) was discovered here. The Ladera Linda Community Center is worth a visit in its own right. The Discovery Room holds assorted skins, fossils, crystals, and bones that children can touch and hold, along with a rabbit, tarantula, snake and mouse (that can also be touched with the staff's assistance). With reservations, the staff at Ladera Linda will take groups on guided walks into the hills around the Center. The Center also is the site for many classes, from ballroom dancing to speed reading, and assorted programs run by the Rancho Palos Verdes Recreation and Parks Department. For more information, call 541-7073.

If you want to **explore the area** around Ladera Linda, walk through the upper parking lot and climb the stairs to the soccer field beyond. The upper two fields belong to the Palos Verdes Peninsula Unified School District, which may put them on the market at some point. (The fields can be rented for soccer and softball games or company picnics; call 541-7073).

The 163 acres of land to the north and east, known as the Forrestal Tract, is privately owned. In 1990 a 43-home development was approved for the 23 acres to the north, with the remaining 140 acres to be donated to the City as parkland. The City also asked the developer to build an extensive trail system and to trim the cliff face to create a gentler slope. In 1992 difficulties with the grading planned for the site caused the plan to be rejected by the City.

To the east of the soccer field part of the cliff face has been covered with sprayed cement. Just to the left of the cement you can see an exposure of purplish **bentonite**, a soft, clay material that causes landslide problems in other areas. The deterioration of the road below the cliff is also due to the swelling of the bentonite.

On the face of the large vertical cliff you can see some grayish-greenish-brownish material. This is **basalt**, an igneous rock that squeezed its way into the sedimentary Altamira Shale. Since it was very hot and liquid at the time, it melted the rock that was already there and changed its chemical composition. This sill (an intrusion between sedimentary beds) is irregular in thickness and has a uniform texture. During the early 50's the basalt was quarried for use in railroad bed material, and many local residents know the site as Livingston Quarries.

If you look carefully in pockets and cracks in the rocks of the Peninsula, you can find **crystals** of dolomite, calcite, barite and quartz, as well as massive gypsum. Here are some tips to identify your treasures:

> **Gypsum** is milky white and is so soft that you can scratch it with your fingernail. It sometimes comes in an exotic curled form, called a Ram's horn, which is quite lovely and very rare.
>
> **Dolomite** is pale beige to pink, with crystals that have a triangular cross section. Calcite is similar but is pale yellow. Both are harder than gypsum but can be scratched with a penknife.
>
> **Quartz** can be white, clear, brown or yellow. It is very shiny, has a six-sided crystal, and breaks leaving smooth hollows. It is very hard and cannot be scratched by a penknife. Quartz is very common and forms beach sand and most white pebbles.
>
> **Barite** forms small flat crystals that are white, pink, or clear. It scratches calcite or gypsum but not quartz.

Many of the rock formations on the Peninsula are composed of thinly-bedded shales, many of which contain **fossils**, particularly fish scales. (Sometimes the rocks are freckled with these scales, which are reddish brown, generally round, and up to the size of a fingernail.) You may see crescent-shaped cross sections of shells, and if you are lucky, you may find a fish skeleton, a leaf or a shark tooth embedded in the rock.

The vegetation is this area is typical of the "**Coastal Sage Scrub**" **habitat**, characterized by dry vegetation in dusty shades of gray and green. To the eye unfamiliar with it, this assemblage of plants may seem unremarkable, but once educated its subtle beauty is very appealing. All of its members are drought tolerant, and most are relatively fire retardant. Many native birds and animals can survive only on the fruits and vegetation of these plants.

The large, dark green shrub that covers the hillsides is called the **lemonade berry bush**. Its flat pink berries have a tart coating that the Native Americans used to make a refreshing drink.

Two different plants, artemesia and salvia, are confusingly called **sagebrush and sage**, but both have a strong sage odor when the leaves are crushed. The sagebrushes are members of the sunflower family, have very narrow grayish-white leaves with a feathery look, and grow from 3-6 feet high. Their tiny flowers are tucked into the base of the leaves.

Both purple and black **sages** are found growing in the canyons. The former has 2-3 foot-long hairy grayish leaves and blue flowers. Black sage has dark green leaves 1-2 inches long and clusters of purple flowers. Both sages form bushes up to six feet high with woody stems. During the dry season the spherical seed pods make a decorative accent on the hillsides.

Sage originated on the northern shores of the Mediterranean and has been cultivated for thousands of years in Europe for its **medicinal values**. Its name, salvia, comes from the Latin "to save". Bees love the plants and sage honey is greatly prized. Sage teas are said to restore energy and bad memory, and to cure indigestion and almost any other disorder, perhaps because of the aromatic oil contained in the leaves. It is also this oil that makes the sage plant quite flammable.

In 1973 almost 900 acres on the south side of the Peninsula

burned, destroying 13 homes and damaging 11 others. **Fire** is much less likely on the Peninsula than in less developed and dryer areas, but it still can be a danger, particularly in canyons where a strong breeze blows off the ocean. Fire officials recommend landscaping with fire-retardant plants in dry areas.

Rocky areas like this are sometimes home to **Pacific Rattlers**, the only poisonous snake in California. It is important to be sensible about snakes: remember that they are just as frightened of you as you are of them. Take care when entering a wild area with rocks, woodpiles, or heaps of debris and brush, because snakes spend their days in that kind of spot. Stamp your feet to alert any snakes to your presence; they are deaf but very sensitive to vibration of the ground.

The rattlers on the Peninsula can be up to three feet in length, with a thick body and up to ten rattles, which they shake when alarmed, making a buzzing noise. During the **winter, snakes** remain in dens in hibernation, coming out in May and June. They hunt at night, eating birds, frogs, lizards, mice and even rabbits, and then rest during the day. Babies are born alive in late summer or early fall and are immediately dangerous. The snakes shed their skins up to three times a year, adding a rattle each time, but they also loose rattles as they age.

Rattlesnakes would prefer not to have anything to do with you. They only rattle if they feel cornered, and only **strike** when they have no other option. If you see or hear a rattlesnake, move away slowly. If you are bitten, chances are very small that you will suffer serious harm. Remain calm and rest, keeping the bitten part still and lower than the heart. Send someone for help. Place a constricting band between the bite and the heart but never use a tourniquet, and do not attempt the "cut and suck treatment. The victim may drink water but no alcohol. Professional medical treatment should be obtained as soon as possible.

The odds against dying from a snakebite are 2 million to one, so there is no need to avoid the outdoors for fear of snakes. Snakes form an important part of the **ecological system,** keeping the rodent population down and providing food for owls, hawks and other, friendlier snakes. Remember when hiking to let the snakes know you're there, and they will stay away from you.

MILEAGE

Drive back down Forrestal Drive and turn left onto Palos Verdes Drive South.　　0
　　.3

(If your time is limited you may want to take a shortened version of the driving tour. If so, turn left after .9 mile onto Palos Verdes Drive East. Stop X, **Short Cut**, will lead you through the cutoff and will return you to the driving tour part way through Stop 8, Gaffey Overlook.)　　.9

The **coastal lands** on your right were approved for development in 1992 by the City, although the Coastal Commission turned the project down. The project included an 18-hole golf course, 84 homes, parkland, and an extensive bicycle and hiking trail network. Revisions to the proposal may make it acceptable to the Commission.　　1.2

The large **white condominium** project was the last building constructed on this stretch of coastline before the incorporation of the city of Rancho Palos Verdes enabled residents to control further building. Much more development was planned, including a large shopping mall and more condominiums.　　1.3

The 53 acres of land just before the border with San Pedro, lower than the land around it, belongs to the County of Los Angeles and is set aside as a passive (undeveloped) park called **Shoreline Park**. It is unbuildable, since it is a landslide, but has been suggested as part of a proposed golf course. At one time the County said that it was for sale but then withdrew the offering. Local conservation groups have offered to manage the parcel as natural open space (and to reintroduce the native coastal grassland habitat), and have suggested renaming it the **South Shores Natural Area**. The coastal bluff habitat in this area is especially varied and significant.　　1.4

Forrestal Drive

MILEAGE	
1.6	As you leave Rancho Palos Verdes and enter San Pedro you will see some mobile homes on the right. This is located on the other half of an ancient landslide known as the **South Shores landslide**. When development began in this area geologists indicated that the land was unstable, but work that was already underway was allowed to continue, and more than 50 permanent homes now lie on this landslide.

Further development was halted and it was decided that the only acceptable use for the remaining land was for **mobile homes**. They could be quickly removed if the slide became active, and the work involved in siting them would lessen the likelihood of a slide. Grading moved some of the weight of the slide from the top and drainage was improved. Residents now hope that their homes never turn out to be truly mobile. |
| 2.5 | *The road you are travelling on becomes 25th Street in San Pedro. Turn right on Western Avenue after 2.5 miles, at the light after the Unocal gas station.*

The housing on your left was developed to keep the aerospace industry a viable part of the South Bay. |
| 3.1 | *Follow Western Avenue. After .6 mile, when Western ends, turn left on Paseo del Mar.* |
| 3.2 | Shortly after the turn you will see on your right a dirt parking area, just before a gated road down to the beach. If you want to visit the beach you can pay the $4 fee and drive down to the bottom where there is parking. If you do not want to pay the fee, park at the top as close to the gate as you can. Walk through the gate and follow the path to the cliff top for a view of White Point and Royal Palms Beach Park.

BE VERY CAREFUL. THE CLIFF IS EXTREMELY STEEP AND THERE IS NO GUARD RAIL! |

◆**Stop X.**

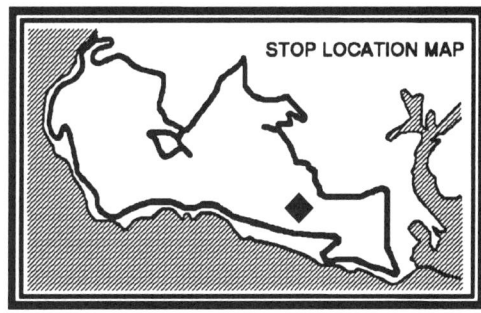

Short Cut

If your time is limited you may want to take an **abbreviated version** of the driving tour. This eliminates Stops 5-8, which take you through some historic parts of San Pedro. Much of the early history of the area is covered in that section of the tour, so it is recommended that you at least read those chapters.

                                                MILEAGE

From the Forrestal Drive stop, return to Palos Verdes Drive South and turn left.   0
.3

After .9 mile bear left onto Palos Verdes Drive East.   1.2

This road rises sharply up the hillside through some spectacular **switchbacks**. These were completed in 1927 and formed part of the new road completely around the outside of the Peninsula. A caravan of three hundred cars descended the hill here in August of 1926 to celebrate the opening of the new road.

From the lookout at the top of the switchbacks you have a splendid view of the coast. The 95-acre parcel below you was given to the City as open space associated with the Sea Bluff development. A group from Marymount College has proposed an ambitious project that would add more than one thousand **trees and native plants** throughout the switchback area.

On the hillsides you will see numerous plants of the **prickly pear cactus**. The stems are from five to ten inches long and flat, with sharp spikes. The yellow flowers come in late spring and are followed by purplish-red fruits sometimes called "cactus apples". They are edible, and can be peeled and then eaten raw or cooked as a vegetable.

Near the prickly pears, you will often find one of the most dangerous of cactus plants, the **"jumping" cholla**. Its tree-like branches are covered with extremely sharp spines that detach themselves at the lightest touch. To make it even nastier, its spines have backwardly-directed barbs that make them difficult and painful to remove from the skin. Because of the fuzzy brown appearance of its branches, the plant is also called the "teddybear cholla", a name that seems cruelly misleading.

You will also see a low, pinkish bush with clusters of flowers or seeds. This is **wild buckwheat**. The leaves are small and pale, the stems are woody, and the flowers or seeds are held in clusters at the top of the stems. This plant is a major food source for butterflies.

The large (up to fifteen feet tall) plants with the deeply lobed dark green leaves are **castor bean plants**. They have both red and cream-colored flowers in April and June, followed by clusters of dark seeds. The seeds are used to make castor oil, an ingredient in slippery potions like laxatives, engine oil, and leather softeners. The entire plant in its natural state, however, is extremely poisonous. One to three seeds can be fatal for a child, and two to eight for an adult. They are non-native, and once introduced into an area will crowd out the local plants.

The plants that line the road are **rabbitfoot grass**, just over a foot tall with two-to-three-inch soft hairy tops.

Other **grasses** include the giant rye grass, up to eight feet tall with a plumed top, and foxtail grass. Wild oats can be very dangerous to animals, for in the same way they work themselves through socks and sneakers, they can work themselves through the skins of dogs, for example. Most grasses are non-native, brought to the Peninsula as food for grazing cattle and spread by the beasts' droppings. Native grasses are more delicate, with graceful arching branches, and can be found in isolated areas.

MILEAGE 2.0 On your right you will pass **Marymount College**, established in 1932 as a two-year college with a liberal arts program. In 1948 it added baccalaureate degrees, and in 1960 moved to the Palos Verdes Peninsula. In 1973 the four-year program merged with Loyola University to form Loyola Marymount University, leaving only the two-year program at the Palos Verdes campus.

Just across from Marymount College, you can take an **interesting detour**. Crest Road leads to San Pedro Hill, the highest point on the Peninsula at 1480 feet, where the white spheres of the radar towers sit. The drive to the top is 1.6 miles, and the views en route of the harbor and city are very impressive. Crest Road actually extends through Rolling Hills to the west side of the Peninsula, but Rolling Hills has chosen not to provide access from the east side.

The **radar towers** sit on an 11.2 acre tract that is jointly occupied by the U.S. Air Force and the Federal Aviation Administration. The towers perform two functions and serve two purposes. First, they provide information to air traffic controllers at LAX Airport some 15 miles to the north. Second, they are one of ten air defense radar systems monitoring U.S. airspace for enemy aircraft. One of the towers measures distance above ground, while the other determines location. They were moved to this site in 1962 from their original site at Camp Cook.

(1.6) *From Crest Road, return to Palos Verdes Drive East, and turn left.*

You rejoin the route of the driving tour toward the end of Stop 8, (Gaffey Overlook) where Miraleste Drive intersects with Palos Verdes Drive East.

3.5 *Continue north to Stop 9, Georgeff Canyon, and stop on the roadside near the Martingale Park sign.*

◆Stop 5.
White Point

From a cliff-top vantage point just past the fountain you can see Royal Palms Beach State Park and the rocky tidal zone. Be very careful - **the cliff is steep** and there is no guardrail. If you venture down to the shore, also be careful climbing on the rocks, particularly if the tide is coming in. Sudden waves regularly sweep people away.

All around you are holes made by **pocket gophers**. These small (6-8" plus a 4" tail) creatures dig elaborate burrows with their strong claws, pushing the dirt out with their heads and forefeet. They eat plant roots, carrying short pieces in their cheek pouches to storage areas underground, and do great damage to vegetation. They reproduce prolifically, providing food for the next step up in the food chain.

This point probably got its name from the sheer **mudstone cliffs** which shine white to ships out at sea. On some maps, however, it is called White's Point, perhaps for an English sailor who jumped ship in the 1800's and was hired by the Sepulvedas. In the cliff to the right you can see some extensively folded beds of Altamira Shale. The smooth black rocks right below are part of a basaltic lava flow, while the rocks used in the breakwater around the lower parking lot are granite, brought from somewhere north of Los Angeles, probably for one of the breakwaters in the harbor. Divers like this area. You can often see classes of rubber-suited men and women lumbering off into the waves.

This beach is one spot where the **grunions** have come, although they really prefer the sandier Cabrillo Beach farther north in the harbor. Grunions are small (6-8") fish that have been described as a cross between a sardine and an anchovy. They frequent the California coast between Baja and Point Concepcion, arriving in huge numbers on sandy beaches just after the monthly highest tides to mate and lay their eggs in the sand. Their silvery bodies gleaming in the moonlight, the females drill a shallow hole in the sand with their tails, laying 1,000 to 3,000 eggs at one time. Male fish circle the females and then emit a milky substance that covers the eggs. Mission accomplished, the grunions head back out to sea, joined some ten days later by their newly-hatched offspring.

On **grunion nights** crowds gather on the beaches to enjoy the spectacle of heaps of shining, wiggling fish. Some people like to catch and cook the grunions, although they can only be caught with bare hands and anyone over 16 must have a valid fishing license.

The cement rectangle between the rocks and the shore below is the only remnant of one of the high points of **Japanese enterprise** in the Peninsula area. After the Sino-Japanese

War (1894-5), eager young Japanese came to America to avoid universal military conscription, high taxation and economic depression. From the very beginning they were not welcomed and efforts were made to limit their numbers.

Nevertheless, a small **colony of Japanese** established themselves here at White Point around the turn of the century. Naked divers harvested abalone with knives, bringing the shellfish back to others on the beach, where they cooked and dried it. By 1903 they had added a canning operation, but a few years later publicity brought public opposition to their presence, and in 1905 the state of California forced them to leave. They returned a few years later, building a larger fishing camp which could be reached by a Red Car line from 'Little Tokyo" in Los Angeles.

Harry Phillips, the manager of the Bixby Ranch on the Palos Verdes Peninsula, encouraged Japanese families to lease land and start **vegetable farms**. The best known local family, the Ishibashis, was established by two brothers who made their way here around 1900 and started farming the Paseo del Mar area. They paid approximately $6 per year in gold for the land to grow beans, peas and tomatoes.

In 1913 Congress passed the Alien Land Law (prohibiting foreigners from owning land), the Bixby family sold its land to Frank Vanderlip, and tuna canneries opened on Terminal Island. All three of these events caused **problems** for the local Japanese. Development began on land they had farmed, and competition with southern European fishermen for the tuna business brought tensions.

In 1917 Tamiji Tagami leased the White Point area from Ramon Sepulveda and constructed a **luxury resort hotel.** Five hot sulphur pools were the main attraction, filled by natural springs. The rectangle below is the foundation for the largest of the pools. There was also a 50-room, two-story hotel, a restaurant, theater, dance floor and enclosed boating area. The fountain now on the cliff top once stood in front of the hotel. A barge was anchored three miles offshore and water taxis brought visitors out to fish. Thousands of Japanese came from all over the southwest to visit the hotel.

While the Japanese enjoyed the resort at White Point, Ramon Sepulveda developed his own resort, called *Royal Palms, The Family Club*, on the beach to the right. A huge, native-rock fireplace was built into the base of the cliff, next to a large terrazzo dance floor. Beautiful gardens stretched along the lower bluff and surrounded a small house.

In 1927 a storm and tidal wave destroyed the wall of the swimming pool, and in 1933 the Long Beach earthquake cut off the flow from the hot springs. These changes and the effects of the Depression caused the hotel to be abandoned. At the outbreak of World War II, the U.S. Navy took over the site and allowed a **demolition team** to practice there.

During the 20's and 30's, more **Japanese farmers** arrived in Palos Verdes, and their children went to school at Malaga Cove. They prospered there; the San Pedro tomato, famous for its flavor and color, was exported as far as the east coast. During the Depression the Japanese farmers were generous with food for the unemployed.

Japanese fishing boats went far down into Mexico and as far north as Point Conception, bringing back a variety of seafood, including tuna, abalone and clams. Most of the catch went to the nine packing houses in San Pedro, which was the center of the area's canning industry. By the 1930's more than 2000 Japanese lived in East San Pedro, with more than 60 stores, a post office, bank, Japanese newspaper, and providers of professional services.

In 1941 the fragile peace between the Japanese and the rest of the Peninsulans was broken. The west coast was declared a theater of war. The Palos Verdes Estates City Council voted that all Japanese be removed from the Peninsula because it was a strategic area. The local Japanese tried to cooperate, but by the following spring their **forced evacuation** was underway.

A few farmers were able to save something by negotiating a deal with a farmer from the Imperial Valley to take over their leases, but others were forced to abandon everything with **no recompense**. Mexican families were moved into the homes

of the Japanese to take over their farms. The local paper did request donations of toys, athletic equipment, games and dolls for the 50 children evacuated, since they had been allowed to take with them only the barest necessities.

The **evacuation camps** were brutal places and the evacuees suffered greatly. In 1943 the U.S. Army formed an all-Nisei (Americans of Japanese descent) brigade and many of the Ishibashi boys joined. In 1945 the exclusion order was lifted, but most Japanese had nowhere to return. Many went east where anti-Japanese bigotry was not so strong. In 1946 a relocation camp was set up at Lomita Field for those who did return, and the local newspaper asked residents to hire them as gardeners or handymen.

Both Mas and James **Ishibashi** returned to the Peninsula in 1947, and began farming peas and garbanzo beans. Today Mas Ishibashi and his son Satoshi farm land near the Marineland site. James and Annie Ishibashi raise strawberries, flowers and vegetables on land near the coast and sell them at the stand you saw outside the Abalone Cove Parking Lot. James Hatano farms land on the Point Vicente Interpretive Center site. However, as development of the farmland continues, however, one of the oldest traditions on the Peninsula may finally die away.

Above the cliffs to the west the Royal Palms Golf and Country Club was established in 1927. The 166-acre site had an elegant 2-storey clubhouse and a par 70, 18-hole course. The club was closed during the Depression and the land was later developed for residential homes.

MILEAGE

0	**Continue east along Paseo del Mar.**
.2	On your left you will pass **White Point Reservation,** once part of the military defenses of the west coast. The large cement construction on the hillside is Battery Paul D. Bunker, built in 1942 to hold two 16-inch guns that could send a 2,340-pound projectile 26 miles.
.9	Across from Barbara Street, **Point Fermin Park** begins on your right. There are lookouts at .1, 1.3, and 1.4 miles, and restrooms and a trail to the beach at 1.1 miles.
	This western section of the park was the site of **Peck's Pavilion**, built in 1908 by George H. Peck, a successful local real estate man, to promote his Ocean View subdivision. A large, many-windowed green building, it held Sunday dances and served as a boxing arena and roller skating rink before it was demolished in 1925.
	On the hillside to your left you can see the **Korean Friendship Bell**, a gift from the people of Korea to commemorate the bicentennial.
1.7	*After 1.7 miles you will come to a stop sign at Gaffey Street. Turn right, past the buoy and anchor display, and park in the lot.*

◆Stop 6.
Point Fermin

This **scenic park** surrounds the southernmost point in Los Angeles County. A stroll through it will show you one of the oldest lighthouses on the west coast, yet another landslide (a different type, at least), the famous Walker's Café, and the headquarters of the American Cetacean Society.

Point Fermin was given its name by the British explorer George Vancouver, who visited here in 1793 and decided to thank Father Fermin Francisco de Lasuen for his hospitality at the Mission in Carmel by naming the point for him.

If you walk to the left along the road you will come to colorful **Walker's Café**, a San Pedro landmark for decades. It was opened in the 1940's by Bessie and Ray Walker as a 14-stool, walk up, outdoor bar called "Cuddles", which Bessie described as "such a dive that roaches walked off with the food, utensils and maybe some customers." Ray died in 1958 but Bessie has continued as "waitress, cook, manager, bouncer, boss and friend." The decor is eclectic clutter, ranging from china figurines to sentimental prints to athletic trophies, and the atmosphere is friendly. Scenes from two movies were filmed at Walker's: *Whatever Happened to the Black Dahlia?* with Efrem Zimbalist, Jr. and Luci Arnez, and *Chinatown*, with Jack Nicholson and Faye Dunaway. Specialties of the house include a BLTA (bacon, lettuce, tomato and avocado) sandwich, and lima beans with sourdough bread.

If you follow the road to the chain-link fence you will see that it ends abruptly. This is the site of the Point Fermin **landslide**, which happened suddenly in 1929 and was reactivated in 1940 and 1941. This is a "glide block" slide, where large pieces of solid rock collapse without breaking up. You can still see the tracks of the streetcar line that ran along Paseo del Mar, and large plates of isolated pavement sitting like caps on top of the blocks.

If you follow the path to the right, toward the point, you will pass a large beige building with a whale painted on its far side. This was once a restaurant and is now a community center and the National Headquarters of the **American Cetacean Society**, an international educational, research, and conservation organization founded in 1967. The Society is one of the oldest of the whale conservation organizations, but differs from some others in that it believes that in the long run the best way to ensure the continued survival of whales and dolphins is through public education. The office coordinates volunteer opportunities, publishes a quarterly journal and a newsletter, and has a research library open to the public.

The **Point Fermin Lighthouse**, the Victorian-style building surrounded by flower gardens, was built in 1874 on three acres of land donated by José Diego Sepulveda. The U.S. government sent him a check for $35, surely a bargain price, which he returned, uncashed. Supposedly this check is still in the Federal archives.

Construction of the lighthouse was inspired by **Phineas T. Banning**, a whiz-kid immigrant from Wilmington, Delaware who began petitioning the government in 1858 to provide assistance to ship traffic around the point. His request for $100,000 was whittled down to $30,000 but was finally approved. The lighthouse was built and opened in 1874 and served as an aid to shipping for nearly a hundred years.

The early history of the Peninsula is very much the story of the **Dominguez and Sepulveda families**, their trials and tribulations, their feuds and friendships. Both families and their names remain an important part of the Spanish heritage of the area.

After Cabrillo's sail up the coastline of California in 1542 and Viscaíno's visit in 1602, the **Spanish** ignored California, concentrating their colonizing efforts on Mexico and the Philippines. It was not until 1770, worried by southward exploration by the British (particularly Vancouver) and the Russians, that the Spanish became concerned with their claim to the land. During the late 1700's a series of missions was established throughout southern California, led by Father Junipero Serra.

In 1784 one of the soldiers who accompanied the missionaries, an experienced man named **Juan José Dominguez**, decided to retire. The new Spanish Governor of California, an old friend of his, gave him permission to use all the land southwest of a line from today's Redondo Beach to Long Beach. He named his 75,000-acre spread Rancho San Pedro and settled in.

When he died in 1809 his estate was taken over by the man named as Executor in his will, **Manuel Gutierrez**, who ran the ranch and acted as if he owned the place for the next 20 years. He expanded the herds and was active in local politics, serving as Mayor of Los Angeles in 1822 and 1823. Around 1810 he gave permission to run cattle on the Peninsula end of the Rancho to a 17-year old boy named **José Dolores Sepulveda**, who may have been a relative. Little did Gutierrez know the problems he was causing and how confusing the history of the next decades would be!

Young José was from a Spanish family of noble blood that had come with the early missionaries. He and his wife **settled in San Pedro**, set up a trading depot, had 12 children (though only 5 survived), and lived as if the land they ranched belonged to them.

Meanwhile, **Cristobal Dominguez**, who was more or less the heir to Juan José Dominguez (the will was somewhat vague about the disposition of the land), was serving as a soldier in San Diego. He was notified of his uncle's will in 1809 but was evidently too busy with his duties at the Presidio to visit Los Angeles. In 1817, however, prompted perhaps by reports that others were occupying the land, he petitioned the Spanish Governor to recognize his claim and remove unauthorized parties. The Governor quickly awarded the Rancho to him and directed that a survey of the land be made.

The **survey** took more than a month and set forth the first exact boundaries, though these were also to be the subject of litigation in later years. (This area must have been a paradise for lawyers.) An agreement was reached with Gutierrez, allowing him to remain on the Rancho for the rest of his life, with the understanding that on his death the estate would revert to the Dominguez family.

In 1825 Cristobal Dominguez died, spelling out once again in his will his claim to Rancho San Pedro. A short time later his family moved north to the Rancho, led by his oldest and very capable son, **Manuel**. Manuel was fluent in Spanish and English and had built himself a substantial home on the eastern slopes of Dominguez Hill by the time he was 22.

On their arrival they were faced once again with the problem of the Sepulvedas, who by that time had a large home and

The Point Fermin Lighthouse needs frequent repainting due to the strong ocean winds.

more than 800 head of cattle in the Peninsula portion of the Rancho, which they had named **Rancho de los Palos Verdes**. José Dolores Sepulveda had been killed by Indians on his way home from presenting a petition regarding his case to the Governor in Monterey, and his ranch was being managed by Gutierrez since the oldest Sepulveda son was less than ten years old.

In 1834 Governor Figueroa reviewed all the **claims** and awarded the entire Peninsula to the Sepulvedas, with the rest of the Rancho San Pedro confirmed as the property of the Dominguez family. In 1839 Gutierrez died, leaving his possessions to the Sepulvedas, but their problems were far from over.

A review by a new Governor resulted in a "**Decree of Ouster**" that same year, requiring them to leave. They filed a cross complaint leading to yet another review (if you're tired of all this, you can imagine how the Sepulvedas felt!), and finally in 1841 the Governor returned to the 1834 decision.

The Sepulvedas' ownership of Rancho de los Palos Verdes was confirmed once again in 1846 by Governor Pio Pico and the controversy seemed to be over. After California became a part of the United States in 1847, the Sepulveda claim to Palos Verdes and the Dominguez claim to San Pedro were both accepted by the Board of Land Commissioners, but **lawsuits** from within and without the families continued to cast doubt on their land-owning rights.

Manuel and Maria Engracia Dominguez retained 30,000 acres to the east, on what was called Rancho San Pedro. Their sons all died young, leaving **six daughters** to inherit equal shares of the Rancho. Ana and Guadalupe died unmarried, so their shares reverted to the Dominguez Estate Company, but the other girls married and their husbands' names are scattered across the South Bay. Dolores married James Watson, Maria Victoria married Henry Carson, Maria Jesus married John Francis, and Susana married Gregorio del Amo.

Things finally fell apart for the Sepulvedas due to the droughts of the 1860's, the severe decline in cattle prices, and the costs of their court battles. They mortgaged their lands and finally were forced to sell all their **Peninsula acreage** in 1882, though the family remained a prosperous part of the San Pedro community.

Most of Rancho de los Palos Verdes was sold to a man named **Jotham Bixby**. Seven hundred acres on Point Fermin went to a German immigrant named Augustus Timms, who built a landing in the harbor, aptly called Timms Landing.

Early in this century **Point Fermin Park** was developed, with gardens, curved pathways and handsome covered picnic areas overlooking the ocean. In the late 1970's the lighthouse was finally closed down, its job taken over by radar and other electronic devices. The building now belongs to the Los Angeles Department of Recreation and Parks and is used as a residence.

The **flower gardens** around the lighthouse are maintained by a Parks Department staffer who brings her pet ducks to keep her company (and eat the slugs) while she creates her floral masterpieces. Controversy arose in 1992 over plans to evict the long-time caretaker in order to convert the historic structure to a museum and wedding chapel.

This park is one of the few places on the Peninsula where **Monarch butterflies** spend the winter, concentrated in clusters on the trees. They summer farther north but cannot survive freezing temperatures, so they head south, their black bordered orange wings making a spectacular display as they gather in a few coastal locations where their food, the milkweed plant, is available.

From the parking lot drive straight north on Gaffey Street for .3 mile. Take your first left into the parking lot for Angel's Gate Park. You will see the Korean Friendship Bell on the hillside to the left.

◆Stop 7.

Angels Gate Park

From the parking lot you can see the Korean Friendship Bell on the knoll before you and the buildings of the former **Upper Reservation of Fort MacArthur** on the slopes behind you. The park's current name came from the opening left in the harbor breakwater when its extension was completed in 1937. Today the two openings, or gates, are called "Queens Gate" (for the one closest to the Queen Mary) and "Angels Gate" (for the one into the port of Los Angeles).

You are standing on the hillside where the ships of Cabrillo may well have spotted the campfires that led them to call the area the "Bay of Smokes" in 1542. It may also have been on this slope, in 1846, that the Mexican soldiers of Carillo tricked the Americans on the beach by marching in circles across the hillsides so that they appeared to be a large and intimidating force. Their ruses were unavailing, however, and in 1847 California became part of the United States. As the port of San Pedro grew, the new government gave thought to the security of its western territories. Land was set aside here in 1888 as a **military reservation** to aid in the defense of the harbor, and additional land on the hillside was purchased in 1906.

Eventually the Fort was to be divided into three sections - the Upper, Middle, and Lower Reservations. In 1914 it was named **Fort MacArthur**, after Arthur MacArthur, a hero of the war in the Philippines (and Douglas's father), and a coastal artillery battalion moved in.

During World War I the Fort served as a training site for thousands of soldiers headed for France. It also became an important part of America's **coastal defense** with the construction, begun in 1916, of Batteries Osgood-Farley, Leary-Merriam, and Barlow-Saxton.

These were massive, 14-inch-**gun emplacements**, concrete platforms protected by walls of 20-foot steel-reinforced concrete on the hillsides. Because the only threat they expected was from the ocean, the guns were mounted on ingenious disappearing carriages that lifted them just long enough to fire. Each gun and carriage weighed 140,000 pounds and shot projectiles that weighed 1560 pounds. Underground concrete bunkers held the ammunition. Each gun cost $165,000, and could be loaded and fired at one-minute intervals, with a range of 17 miles. Further up the slope a battery of 12-

inch mortars could send a 700-pound shell twelve miles out to sea.

Today you can still visit these emplacements, although the guns were removed after World War II. If you walk toward the northwest, past the barracks which now serve as an international youth hostel and a cultural center, you will see the two semicircular cement **Osgood-Farley batteries**. On Saturdays and Sundays from 12:00 to 5:00 you can visit the free Fort MacArthur Military Museum, located in the storage rooms between the two emplacements. During those hours it is also possible to drive directly to the museum (by entering the second driveway into the park) and park in its lot.

The Military Museum has displays and souvenirs of the war eras, diagrams and maps of the reservations, and historical information on the war and its effect on California. The museum continually seeks to expand its collection of documents and records. A walking tour leaflet explains many features of the batteries, like the plotting room, the Commander Station (with rows of functioning speaking tubes that connect to other rooms - great for kids), and the long, narrow tunnels that pass between the various rooms. The underground parts of the battery can only be visited when the museum is open, but much can be seen above ground.

During the late 1920's additional firepower was added to the fortification. Two mobile 14-inch **guns** were mounted on railroad gun carriages, and tracks were constructed across the Middle Reservation. Fake buildings at either end of the track hid the guns from enemy airplanes. When they were fired for the first time in 1927, the shock waves broke windows all over the city. Today all traces of these guns are gone.

If you walk past the Korean Friendship Bell toward the ocean and down the hillside, you will see a round cement platform. This is a "Panama Mount", on which a **mobile gun**, called a "Long Tom" rotated in a circle. This was constructed in 1928 for guns purchased from the French, and was called Battery Hogsdon. Further down the hillside you can see a cement observation bunker sticking up about a foot out of the ground. This was built around 1915 and contained a rotating wooden seat and viewing and plotting instruments.

By 1941 airpower had become an important factor in America's defense and **anti-aircraft guns** were added to strengthen Fort MacArthur. Additional batteries with overhead protection were constructed all along the coast. Also below the Friendship Bell, to the east, is Battery 241, the last one constructed at the Fort (built in 1944). This held two six-inch steel turret guns that weighed 22,000 pounds each and cost $120,000. Today the concrete walls and heavy steel doors of the bunker overlook a small playground and picnic area.

Since the **guns on the site** had become **obsolete** by the end of World War II, they were all cut up for scrap. Fort MacArthur became a Separation Center for returning servicemen. In 1954 the Fort was used as a Nike-Ajax Missile Base. In 1974 much of the Fort was declared surplus and

Range markers are still displayed on the battery walls.

transferred to the L.A. Harbor Department, the L.A. Department of Recreation and Parks, and the L.A. Unified School District. In 1976 Battery Osgood-Farley was placed on the National Register of Historic Places.

Today an enthusiastic volunteer group, called the **Fort MacArthur Military Museum Association** (for information write to 3601 Garrey Street, Battery Osgood-Farley, San Pedro, 90731) works to operate and expand the museum and restore some of the old fortifications. They are also attempting to raise money to bring the only remaining example of the type of gun that was at Osgood-Farley from Corregidor in the Philippines to Fort MacArthur.

As you walk back up the hill you will pass the "**Bell of Friendship**", donated to the United States by the people of Korea as a Bicentennial gift. It is patterned after the largest Oriental bell in existance, the bronze bell of King Songdok, made in 771. A group of more than 20 Korean craftsmen under the direction of a famous sculptor took more than six months to cast the bell. The Korean workers who built the ornate pavilion that holds the bell lived in the Osgood-Farley barracks.

On the sides of the bell the Statue of Liberty is paired four times with a Korean spirit, to **symbolize friendship** between the two nations. They stand on drifting clouds and the sun appears between their raised hands. Each Korean spirit holds a different item; a Korean flag, a branch of Rose of Sharon (Korea's national flower), a laurel branch, and a dove. Relief work showing the Rose of Sharon decorates the rim of the bell. Brilliantly-colored Korean-style painting covers the inside roof and supports of the pavilion.

Designed to hang low to the ground, the bell has a **sound** tube extending from the top to carry its reverberations outward. Underneath there is a hollow, tile-lined area which enables the **vibrations** to be felt as long as five minutes after it is struck with its log striker.

Originally Griffith Park was chosen as the site for the bell, but once this hillside was proposed all involved felt that it was more suitable. The myriad government agencies involved worked to arrange for its location overlooking Los Angeles Harbor so it could serve as the **Statue of Liberty of the Pacific**.

When the bell was dedicated in 1976, it was struck 13 times, to symbolize the 13 colonies, and it is still sounded on July 4, August 15 (Korean Independence Day) and New Year's Day. The Korean Friendship Bell **Information Center** (the small building behind the parking lot) has rotating exhibits and information on the construction of the bell provided by the Korean Consulate. It is open from 10-6 every day. The gardens around the bell are maintained by volunteers from the local Korean community.

Many other **groups** and organizations share Angels Gate Park. The Belmont Shores Railroad Club has an "N-scale" railroad system in one of the barracks, open to the public on Tuesday evenings from 6:30 to 10:00.

The **Marine Exchange** (high on the hill, not open to the public) is the control tower for the port of Los Angeles.

Beyond the Military Museum is the **Marine Mammal Care Center** which rehabilitates injured seals, sea lions and other animals rescued from the ocean. For information or to volunteer, call 548-5677.

In the near future a **memorial** to those who fought in the Korean War will be constructed on the hillside. Paid for exclusively by donations, the monument will have ten life-sized figures of soldiers resting after a battle. Twenty feet away, the figure of a military nurse will reach out towards the men.

The **Angels Gate Cultural Center** is a nonprofit, multidisciplinary, multicultural arts center open from 11-4 Wednesday through Sunday. The Center has an outdoor amphitheater and a gallery (in building A) which hosts changing exhibits. It has an active calendar of events and special programs, and publishes a journal and newsletter. Its jazz concerts, held in an outdoor amphitheater, are a popular yearly event.

Leave the parking lot and turn left onto Gaffey Street. Turn right after .1 mile (at the top of the slope) into the harbor overlook.

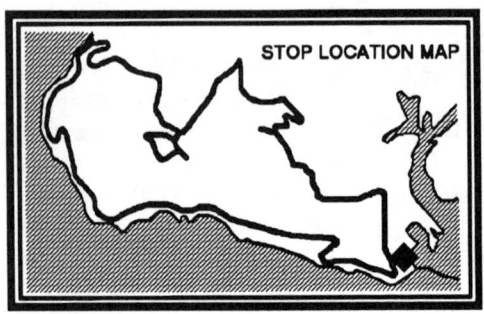

◆Stop 8.

Gaffey Street Overlook

From this location you have a panoramic **view** of San Pedro and the harbor. To your left you can see the Vincent Thomas Bridge which in 1963 replaced the ferry service which had linked the two sides of the harbor. It was criticized for being a "bridge to nowhere" when it was built, but today it is a vital part of the L.A. freeway system. The first bridge built entirely on pilings, it was also the first to be welded rather than riveted. The towers are 35 stories high, and the bridge allows a ship 18 stories-high to pass underneath at high tide.

Over to the right you can see the sweep of the breakwater that encloses the outer harbor, and just above its shoreward end, the **Cabrillo Marine Museum**, an excellent place to learn more about the natural history of the area. The rectangular point across the main harbor channel is Terminal Island, site of a Federal Correctional Institution, an Immigration Station, and a U.S. Coast Guard Base.

Los Angeles harbor, located in San Pedro, is the busiest on the west coast - closely followed by Long Beach Harbor, its other half. Eighty steamship lines bring more than 100,000 tons of cargo over its wharves every day. For statistic lovers, it has 28 miles of waterfront, 7,500 acres of land and water including 200 acres of shed and warehouse space, terminals for all types of commodities, and 33 huge container cranes.

The harbor began as a **mud flat**. Point Fermin and Catalina Island provided some protection from bad weather, making this the best place for ships to stop between San Diego and Monterrey. It was the vision and perseverance of Phineas T. Banning that transformed the area into a viable port. In fact, it has been said that "the history of San Pedro and Wilmington, California *is* the history of Phineas Banning."

When **Phineas Banning** came to California from Wilmington, Delaware in 1851, he was only 21 years old. There were a few docks but the bay was too shallow for cargo ships, which had to anchor a mile off shore. Small boats, called "lighters" transported goods from ship to shore.

Banning got a job in one of the **earliest warehouses** (called the Hide House) and quickly became a partner in the business. He set up a stagecoach line, with 500 mules, 40 horses, freight wagons, and coaches, and indulged himself with stagecoach races against the rival line, owned by Augustus Timms. In 1853 he imported elegant Concord coaches (which cost an incredible $1,000 each) and invited more than two thousand guests to a July 4th celebration. (This man knew how to throw a party.) He also built his own docks and buildings so that when the notification came that San Pedro had been declared an official Port of Entry in 1853, he was ready with the first Customshouse to handle the additional trade.

Banning was ready but the harbor was not. Rattlesnake

Island was a long, thin stretch of land that blocked the mouth of the harbor. In 1854 he and a group of his friends bought 2400 acres of mudflat behind the island and began dredging the harbor, much to the derision of many members of the community who called it "**Banning's Folly**". Three years later he opened his new headquarters, wharf and warehouses in the inner harbor, sheltered from the open ocean though still not accessible to big ships.

Banning seemed untouched by the depression of the 1860's that did the Sepulvedas in. He became the **transportation king of Southern California**, with wagon trains traversing the southwest. He started an oil company and built himself a magnificent mansion that still stands (and is open to the public) in Wilmington. Even though it would hurt his profitable lighterage (ship to shore transportation) business, he began lobbying for Federal money to improve the harbor, and introduced a bill into the California State Legislature (where he was a Senator) to bring a railroad line from Los Angeles to San Pedro.

Banning managed to get his bill through the legislature, then bid on and won the project himself. In 1869 the first engine, called the "Los Angeles" travelled the new **Los Angeles-San Pedro Railroad Line**. Due to his efforts, the U.S. Army Corps of Engineers came out to survey the harbor and recommended the construction of a breakwater between Rattlesnake Island and Deadman's Island (a chunk of rock near the tip of where Terminal Island now stands). Work began two years later, with 600 men using seven steam-powered pile drivers. By 1880 a 4,700-foot bulkhead of heavy timbers and a 2,000-foot stone jetty had been built and the inner harbor was open for business.

Meanwhile, the politics of the railroads had been heating up. Early reports showed that the cost of linking Los Angeles to the transcontinental line would be enormous, but for the port to grow such a link was essential. Southern Pacific, owned by Huntington, Stanford, Hopkins and Crocker, was willing to make a deal - they would get $600,000, free downtown land for the terminal, and all the stock in the L.A.-San Pedro railroad in return for a link to

Many cruise ships (including the "Love Boat") are based in San Pedro.

the Southern Pacific Line. This was accepted but the city then became a prisoner of **Southern Pacific's greed**. Freight rates were raised so high that it cost more to ship goods from San Pedro to L.A. than from the Orient to San Pedro. Attempts to compete with Southern Pacific at Redondo Beach and Santa Monica with ocean piers were driven out of business.

Phineas Banning died in 1885, from injuries received in a fall from a cable car in San Francisco, without seeing his dream of a major harbor in San Pedro come true. He did, nevertheless, have a profound **affect on** the **history** of the Peninsula - by founding the neighboring city of Wilmington, working to develop the port of San Pedro, and establishing reliable transportation lines between Los Angeles and San Pedro.

After his death **conflict over the harbor** escalated. A group of businessmen from St. Louis built a rail line from L.A. to Long Beach, with a spur going out to the end of Rattlesnake Island (renamed Terminal Island). Huntington became President of the Southern Pacific Railroad and, angry at the competition, decided that Santa Monica, where he had complete control, should be the port of Los Angeles. He had a wharf almost a mile long built, with an 800-ton-capacity coal bin at its tip.

In 1893 the U.S. Congress appropriated three million dollars for **port construction**, initially awarded to Santa Monica. After an exciting three-day debate in the U.S. Senate between Senator Frye of Maine (who was an ally of Huntington and supported Santa Monica) and Senator White of California (who favored San Pedro), the money was awarded in true government fashion to whichever port an independent commission would choose.

Huntington went into action, influencing Federal officials, sending fraudulent telegrams to the Commission and using the press to drum up support. After a long and bitter controversy, however, the **"Free Harbor Contest"** was finally decided in favor of San Pedro.

On April 26, 1899, more than 20,000 people gathered to watch as the first barge-load of rock was dumped into the harbor to begin the 9,250-foot **breakwater**. A wooden trestle was built to carry railway flatcars filled with a total of three million tons of granite out ever farther. Dredging of the inner harbor increased its depth to 18 feet.

Building the facilities the new port would need would be an expensive business, and neither **San Pedro** nor Wilmington had the financial resources. In 1909 both cities voted **to merge with** the city of **Los Angeles** so that its municipal funds could help develop the harbor.

On the ocean side of Terminal Island was a very popular strip of sand called **"Brighton Beach"**, with amusement parks and resort hotels. Development put it out of business in the early part of the century, as oil companies and the shipping industry moved in.

The **harbor** continued to grow and change. In 1908 Teddy Roosevelt's *Great White Fleet* with its 16 battleships caused tremendous excitement during its visit to San Pedro. The opening of the Panama Canal in 1914 increased traffic. World War I brought ship-building contracts and a gun emplacement on Deadman's Island. The development of Fish Harbor brought immigrants from Portugal, Scandinavia, Yugoslavia, Italy and Greece, lending a European flavor to the port. In 1929 Deadman's Island was blown up to widen the harbor entrance.

San Pedro suffered during **the Depression**. Labor unrest caused repeated strikes, including one in 1934 in which two men were killed on what was called *Bloody Tuesday*. Federal money started construction on the middle breakwater in the harbor.

In 1940 **Vincent Thomas** was elected to the California Assembly on a platform of secession, with the slogan "I hate Los Angeles". He served for 38 years and although secession is a recurrent issue in local politics, San Pedro still remains part of the city of Los Angeles. Thomas's concern for the needs and development of the harbor caused the authorities to name the new suspension bridge crossing the harbor for him.

World War II brought the **naval shipyard** to San Pedro, with nearly 90,000 people employed. After the war the harbor was dredged to 47 feet to accommodate the new **supertankers** with their cargos of oil, new oil farms were constructed, and the last section of breakwater was built.

In the 1956 the harbor underwent another major change with the opening of the first **container transport** system. Before containers a crew of ten dockworkers could offload ten tons an hour; after containerization, five men could handle 450 tons an hour. With the reduction in manpower the character of the city changed. No longer were there hoards of sailors roaming the streets and making San Pedro somewhat of a frontier town.

Plans for future development are laid out in the Worldport LA's 2020 Program. It call for 1,000 acres of new land created from Outer Harbor dredging, two new piers and development of a transportation route between the port and downtown LA called the Alameda Corridor.

Other projects include a recreation area centered around the Cabrillo Marina; a new fire boat center, freezer warehouse and tourist village called Fisherman's Wharf; and a Cruise Center that can accommodate five ships. Habitat reconstruction at Batiquitos Lagoon (near Carlsbad) and the Cabrillo Salt Marsh, along with kelp reintroduction in the harbor and protection of a tern nesting colony will offset environmental impacts of the expanded port.

MILEAGE

0 *Return to Gaffey Street and drive north for 1.6 miles.*

.1 On your left is Fort MacArthur. Just across from 30th Street you will drive over one of the **buried tunnels** that connect the upper and lower sections of the fort. These were explored recently after the discovery of some old maps that showed the network of tunnels that once underlay the area, but they are in bad condition and dangerous.

Gaffey Street is named for **John T. Gaffey**, an active proponent of harbor development, who was involved in state politics and married Arcadia Bandini, daughter of one of the oldest California families. In 1905 he founded the Pacific Wharf and Storage Company which had docks on Terminal Island and in Wilmington.

.7 At **25th and Gaffey** you will pass the point of a World War II observation post. Just down the hill to the right is Harbor View Memorial Park, where many members of the Sepulveda family are buried and Rudecinda Sepulveda's ornate tomb is located. It is also the site of San Pedro's first church, Saint Peter's Episcopal Church, built in 1884 and moved to this site in 1956.

1.6 *Turn left on 9th Street at the light.*

3.1 *Follow 9th Street west for 2.8 miles, across Western Avenue. It will change its name to Miraleste Drive after it crosses Western.*

The east side of the Palos Verdes Peninsula was named "**Miraleste**" or "look to the east" by those who planned the development of the Peninsula in the early 1920's. The same architectural criteria were applied to the homes built in Miraleste, which was part of the Homes Association. After the Depression the Homes Association was in serious financial difficulties, which were resolved in 1939 when Palos Verdes Estates voted to become a city. Since the land in Miraleste was not contiguous with the new city, it could not be included. It was not until Rancho Palos Verdes was formed in 1973 that Miraleste became part of an incorporated city.

MILEAGE

Turn right onto Palos Verdes Drive East. (This is where drivers taking the Short Cut will rejoin the driving tour.) Continue for .7 mile. 4.4

You will pass **Miraleste Intermediate School**, part of the Palos Verdes Peninsula Unified School District. This school was a high school until 1991, when, because of declining enrollment the School Board voted to consolidate the three high schools into one and chose the most centally located facility as the new high school. 4.6

Turn left onto Bronco Drive and go .3 mile to Martingale Park, on the right side overlooking the canyon. You will see a water fountain/watering trough. Park by the roadside. 5.1

5.4

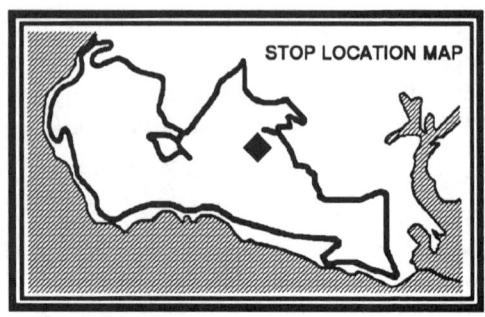

◆ **Stop 9.**

Georgeff Canyon

From this overlook you can see into George F. (or Georgeff, or Georgette) **Canyon**, which drains the northeast side of the Peninsula, down to the reservoir area. The origin of its name is somewhat of a mystery. It may have been mistakenly named for George H. Bixby, since an early photograph called it Bixby Canyon, or it may have been named for George F. Vickery, a wholesale butcher in San Pedro in the 1900's.

Martingale Park was created in the late 80's to protect access to the trails for residents of this neighborhood. It has a cleverly-designed water fountain for people and horses.

Across the valley is the City of Rolling Hills. You can see the extensive canyon-side gardens and orchards of one Rolling Hills resident, who has a funicular railroad to access the lowest fruit groves.

If you feel like stretching your legs, you can walk (approximately one mile, round trip) down into the canyon to see one of the few exposures of the **oldest rock** on the Peninsula, the Catalina Schist. Walk down Bronco Drive and then turn left and walk down Cayuse Lane. Turn left on Chaparral Road and walk to the end. There is space to park there but it is a private road. A path leads over a small rise, where you can examine an outcrop of the schist, a very hard, brown rock in tight rippled beds.

From the overlook you can see exposures of the schist in the canyon wall opposite. It's an unusual rock, called a **glaucophane schist**, named for a rare bluish mineral it contains. It is approximately 130 million years old, deposited during the age of the dinosaurs (though no dinosaur fossils are present) and since then has been melted and compressed so that no traces of its original structure remain. The caves you see were probably put to use by the area's earliest residents.

These canyons are home to many **wild animals**. Coyotes, early residents of the Peninsula, have probably been driven out by development, although occasional sightings in the wilder canyons are still reported. Wild dogs can cause problems as they forage for food, and coys, crosses between coyotes and dogs, may be living in the remote canyons. The native gray fox is seldom seen, but red foxes, introduced by early hunters, are occasionally spotted in the hills.

Animals that can coexist successfully with development are the most common on the Peninsula, like racoons, possums and skunks. **Raccoons**, with their masked faces and characteristic ringed tails, raid trash cans and sleep in hollow trees, caves or attics. Baby raccoons are born in April and are raised by both parents.

The common skunk is a frequent evening stroller across the streets of Palos Verdes. They live in holes in the ground and eat bugs and grubs, small animals, pet food and garbage. If you spot one of these small black creatures with the black stripe down its back, don't stand behind it when it lifts its tail, for it can shoot a squirt of strong, repulsive liquid up to 12 feet when it feels threatened.

Opossums sleep in the trees during the day and spend their nights hunting for eggs, fruit, mice and insects. They are cat-sized, with grayish fur and a long, ratlike tail. Their babies (up to 20 per litter, although there are only 13 teats so only that many will survive) are born smaller than a honeybee and spend their first two months of life in a pouch on the mother's stomach.

MILEAGE

0   **Return down Bronco Drive to Palos Verdes Drive East.**

.2

On your right, across from Cayuse Lane, the rubbly rock wall is the exposed face of the **Cabrillo Fault**, which extends from Point Fermin to a spot just northwest of here. Another fault, called the Palos Verdes Fault, parallels this one just to the northeast and separates the Peninsula from Los Angeles. The rock exposed here is the Altamira Shale, thin brown beds of mudstone around 30 million years old.

Palos Verdes may be one of the best places in California to be when the big **earthquake** comes, since most of the land has rock very close to the surface. When earthquake waves travel through solid rock, the ground shakes but vibrations are not transmitted as readily into buildings and the damage is less severe.

.3   **Turn left onto Palos Verdes Drive East and go 2.2 miles.**

1.9   On your right is the Palos Verdes **Reservoir**. Rainfall on the Peninsula averages from 11 to 15 inches per year and is seasonal, making it a natural dry or semi-arid desert. Bringing a reliable supply of water here was therefore essential before any development could occur. The story of water on the Peninsula is an important factor in its history.

MILEAGE
1.9

The Native American villages on the Peninsula depended on springs that flowed in the canyons and on lakes that filled clay-bottomed depressions during the rainy season, but these dried up in years of drought and would not support a large population. The closest major **source of water** was the Los Angeles River, which today flows to the ocean just west of Long Beach. In earlier days its course varied, leaving a remnant behind in what is today called Harbor Lake. The largest Indian villages and the early colonists all gathered in this area, at the northeast corner of the Peninsula.

When José Dolores Sepulveda rode to Monterrey to file his claim to the Peninsula in 1824, he submitted a map of the rancho that clearly showed **springs and a lake**. During the drought of 1862-64, however, the springs dried up and cattle on the Sepulveda Ranch died by the thousands, leading to the eventual loss of the land by the Sepulvedas.

It was Phineas T. Banning, ever the entrepreneur, who first had the idea of using his oil drilling rig to drill successfully for **artesian water**. When the planners of the Palos Verdes Project decided to develop the area in the early 1900's they looked to this artesian source to provide their water. A series of pumping stations was set up to lift the water to tanks on the hills where gravity would provide water pressure. In keeping with the aesthetic goals of the project, the tanks were buried underground and the pumping stations were skillfully landscaped.

The cost of such beautification was high and money was saved by making the **water mains of wood**en

MILEAGE 1.9 staves bound together with steel hoops. This system began to fail right in the middle of the Depression, when there was no money available for repairs. The water began to look and taste quite dubious. Finally, the water company was turned over to some local businessmen for free, if they would only solve its problems. The Doty brothers relaid over two million feet of pipe, using surplus oil line pipe that they had sterilized by burning off the oil. They had no trouble locating the old line, since it was overgrown by swamps of cattails enjoying the steady supply of water leaking from the mains.

Eventually the company became solvent. It was sold to Great Lakes Carbon, who had been mining diatomite on the Peninsula, and then to its present owners, the **California Water Service Company.**

By the early 1950's population growth in Los Angeles had **depleted** the **artesian water** so much that sea water began to flow into the wells. It was necessary to purchase Owens and Colorado river water from the Metropolitan Water District. A barrier was constructed to keep the sea water from the artesian layer, and fresh water was injected back underground along the seaward edge of the aquifer in an immense project carried out in the late 60's.

MILEAGE

Today about 70% of the Peninsula water comes from the Colorado River, and 30% from northern California and the Feather River project. The Metropolitan Water District delivers it to this reservoir, from which it is pumped to other, smaller reservoirs. The reservoir is **covered** to cut down on evaporation and keep the water clean.

The water that gets to the Peninsula, like most city water, is very alkaline and very hard. In fact, the water company calls it "**aggressive water**" because of the difficulties it causes. Water rates are higher here than in other parts of the country because of the difficulty in bringing water to L.A. and because of the additional unique problems of Palos Verdes; laying pipe on the Peninsula is expensive since the ground is often hard rock which must be blasted, water must be pumped up five levels to serve the highest residents, and pipes on the Portuguese Bend landslide are above ground and must be inspected every day for problems that might cause a break.

Turn left onto Palos Verdes Drive.   **2.1**

On your right you will pass Dapplegray School. This closed former intermediate school is on a 43-acre site. A proposal for residential development on the site was approved by the Rolling Hills Estates Planning Commission but community pressure caused the application to be withdrawn and the City Council rezoned the site as institutional. Now it is being refurbished for use by a childrens' theater group and as a community center.   **2.7**

Continue on Palos Verdes Drive North. Turn right into the parking lot for the Rolling Hills General Store, immediately after the light at Rolling Hills Road.   **3.1**

Georgeff Canyon

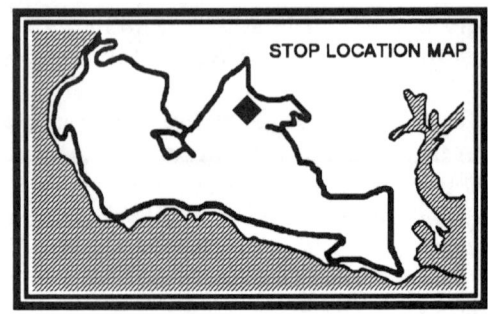

◆Stop 10.
The General Store

This small shop selling souvenirs, snacks and equestrian items is across the street from the main entrance to the city of **Rolling Hills**. Just outside that entrance is a plaque installed by the Rancho de los Palos Verdes Historical Society to commemorate the original gatehouse of the city of Rolling Hills. A second marker, on the site of the Phillips homestead, is located on Rolling Hills Road.

When the Sepulvedas sold their land in the mid-1800's, the largest portion, some 16,000 acres, was bought by Jotham

Bixby. The **Bixby family** were an adventurous bunch. Eight brothers and two sisters emigrated from Maine to California, the last arriving in 1862. They began by looking for gold and were successful in a number of business enterprises, finally settling down to ranching and farming. Undeterred by the difficulties involved, in 1852 three of the brothers sailed east and brought herds of improved varieties of sheep and cattle overland to California.

Jotham Bixby ran some **cattle and sheep** on the Peninsula but lived at Los Cerritos and did little more with the land. He is said to have had a ranch where the Peninsula Center is now, where cattle were claimed in a yearly area-wide rodeo.

Harry Phillips, a young mining engineer who had spent years searching the canyons for water sources, was responsible for the rancho's success. When George Bixby inherited the land from his father in 1894 he hired Phillips to manage the ranch. Phillips improved the herds, bringing in thoroughbred Hereford bulls. He built his first house near the Rolling Hills Estates City Hall and began raising barley and lima beans. He planted eucalyptus trees along the north border of the estate for wood for railroad ties, but the trees grew very quickly and their wood proved too soft. Eighteen vaqueros were employed during the spring roundup in 1911, the next-to-the-last one held on the ranch.

The Farmery, the Phillips' second home, was located behind the General Store, across from where the Empty Saddle Club is now on a spot where a spring once provided water. It had four bedrooms for his family of four children, and numerous outbuildings. A photograph on display at PVIC shows the Phillips family posed before their home, the vaqueros ready for the round-up, and neatly fenced herds on empty plains. In 1913 the Bixbys sold their land and the era of the ranchos was over.

In 1931 the Palos Verdes Project hired as General Manager a man called A.E. Hansen, who had worked as a city planner and landscape architect and who would almost singlehandedly create his own perfect community, **Rolling Hills**. In 1932 he discovered an old ranch house that had been abandoned for more than 40 years on the top of the Peninsula. He moved his family out from Beverly Hills for the summer, rented a cow (possibilities for a franchise?), and began to rebuild the ranch.

Hansen loved the life he led at what he dubbed Rancho Elastico (his son remarked that the land stretched like a rubber band), and after a few years he determined to attract others interested in the same rural values to buy land on the Peninsula. His first campaign, "**Buy Your Own Dude Ranch**", was unsuccessful, probably because few people had the funds in the 30's to purchase the 10 to 50-acre ranches he had in mind.

A new campaign offering one to five-acre lots was more successful. He enlisted the help of Harry Cheney, a nationally known city planner instrumental in the early development of Palos Verdes Estates, and built a gate-house to ensure the privacy he thought was so important to country living. There wasn't much money to spend on development, but he was very **creative**: he had the electric lines installed free because the houses would be "all-electric," and found a contractor who would put in the road in exchange for rock from the quarry. He talked the government into paying 300-400 men with picks and shovels to extend Palos Verdes Drive East, thus providing access to his new development.

The original gate-house stood on a spot just north of the present gate. It had an apartment for the watchman and a sales office, and served as a model building for the project. All the **houses** were required to be one level, painted white, and have a shingle or shake roof. All the ranchitos, as they were called, also had to have a white, three-rail fence surrounding the property. Space was left between all the lots for bridle trails. An entire orchard of olive trees was purchased and transplanted to the hilltop, along with pepper trees and thousands of shrubs.

Inspired by a visit to Colonial Williamsburg in Virginia, Mr. Hansen invited architect Paul Williams to design 14 homes to line **Williamsburg Lane**. These three-bedroom, two-bath homes on one-acre lots sold for $8750.

Homes in the Flying Triangle landslide

On another piece of land south of Crest Road, a group of 35 homes was constructed, taking its name from a branding iron once used by Lewellen Bixby. The three-sided iron had one side shaped like a seagull, so it was called the Flying Triangle. Today this area has problems with landslides and thus is flying in more ways than one.

Money was scarce and taxes went unpaid. In 1939 Hansen tried to get the County to take all the land between Point Vicente and San Pedro to develop as a recreation area in return for writing off $125,000 in delinquent taxes but was unsuccessful. He ran advertisements offering 25-acre parcels for $185 per acre, one-third cash down, but didn't sell any. Other ads featured **The World's Happiest Horse**, *Banjo* and *Jock, the Scottie*, boasting about how happy their masters were with their idyllic lives in Rolling Hills. These ads were more successful, bringing a small but steady number of families.

When Palos Verdes Estates became a city, Rolling Hills was not included. Finally in 1957 residents incorporated to protect the **rural character** of their community. Since all their roads are private, the city can and does prevent access to the entire area.

MILEAGE	
0	From the parking lot, turn left onto Rolling Hills Road and go .9 mile.
.3	You will pass on your left the marker commemorating the site of the **Phillips Ranch**.

.4	**Riding** has always been an important part of Peninsula life. Miles of trails traverse all four Peninsula cities, passing between houses and across parklands. Just past the marker, on your right, is the **Empty Saddle Club**, founded by early residents of Rolling Hills to provide a track, polo club, and rodeo field. One early immigrant from Virginia, a Mrs. French, brought a pack of hounds and stimulated local interest in the hunt. Although live foxes could not be used, a bag holding fox droppings was dragged across the countryside to provide a scent for the trackers. For several years an enthusiastic group participated but eventually the hunt died out.

There are a number of different **trees** that grow along the roads in Palos Verdes. Among the most striking are the **eucalyptus**, varieties of a tree native to Australia. The first ones were planted in 1856 and were so successful that now more than 150 types of eucalyptus have been introduced to every corner of the state. The trees are drought-tolerant, fast growing (some types as much as 10-15 feet per year), and very beautiful. Varieties range from small weeping types to spectacular flowering trees.

MILEAGE

For many years only eucalyptus seeds were imported. No American insects or diseases attacked the trees so they were virtually trouble free. Recently, however, the **eucalyptus longhorn beetle** has made its way to California. This creature has four stages - eggs, larvae, pupae and adult beetles, and spends most of its life inside the tree where pesticides can't reach it. Strong healthy trees produce sap that smothers the beetle larvae, so the key to keeping trees beetle-free is to make sure they have the right amount of water and are pruned properly. To prevent the dispersal of these pests, the State has made the transport of infected eucalyptus wood illegal.

Another common tree is the **pepper tree**, which appears in two quite different forms. The California pepper tree has gnarled, heavy trunks, with thick limbs and drooping, bright green foliage. It is prized for its vibrant color and hardiness but disliked for its intrusive roots that destroy roads. The Brazilian pepper tree has upright branches and darker leaves. It makes an excellent shade tree and in winter has attractive bright red berries.

At the light, turn left onto Crenshaw Boulevard. .9

Go .5 mile and turn left into the South Coast Botanic Garden. 1.4

Botanic Garden — Page 80

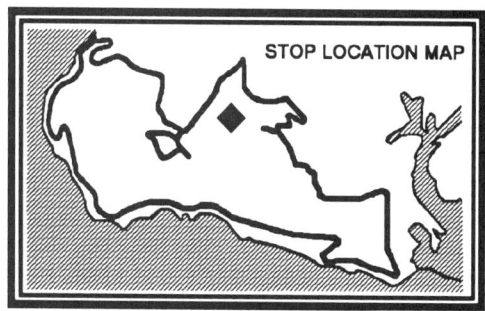

◆Stop 11.

The South Coast Botanic Garden

The Botanic Garden is a public facility owned by the County of Los Angeles Department of Arboreta and Botanic Gardens. Its 87 acres include a lake, desert garden, rose garden, volunteer garden, and tram. **Admission** to the gift shop is free; admission to the garden is $3.00 for adults, $1.50 for seniors over 62 and students, and $.75 for children 5-12. Outside, near the parking lot, there are picnic tables.

A dedicated group of volunteers do much of the work that keeps the Garden a major asset to the community, providing more than 25,000 volunteer hours per year. The vegetable garden is a completely volunteer effort, providing vegetables for the meals on wheels program as well as a decorative garden area. An active education program provides ongoing classes, an outreach program, craft workshops and cultural activities. The gift shop is staffed and run by volunteers, as are the regular plant sales offering unusual and drought-tolerant varieties to area gardeners.

An ambitious $2 million Master Plan for the future has involved local businesses and the community in improving the garden's **facilities**. A new tram is operating, and the first phase of a new Rose Garden is complete, with 1500 roses planted (and there are a few roses bushes still available for

sponsoring). The next project is a garden for the senses, a half-acre of plants with interesting smells and textures. Future plans call for a fuchsia garden, expansion of the gift shop, a drought-tolerant garden, a plaza and fountain, an interpretive center and a butterfly house.

The story behind the Botanic Garden actually begins millions of years ago. This area was once an ocean, filled with tiny, one-celled algae called diatoms. When they died their shells of silica sank to the bottom and were preserved in a deposit known as **diatomaceous earth**. Eventually the land in Palos Verdes rose above sea level, leaving these deposits exposed.

During the early 1900's the Dicalite Company began **mining** the diatomaceous earth, but it was not until 1944 when the area was purchased by the Great Lakes Carbon Company that large-scale mining began. Because the material was very clean, hard, and fine-grained, the deposits were valuable for industrial and chemical applications: as a filtering agent for swimming pools, as an ingredient for abrasives, and as a heat insulator for pipes carrying extremely hot liquids.

By 1956 the deposits were largely mined out and the Great

Lakes Carbon Company moved to Lompoc, having sold the site to the County of Los Angeles to take care of the county's growing **landfill needs**. From the very beginning, the County planned to utilize the best possible technology and to reclaim the land for future use.

There were three parts to the landfill. The section on which you are standing was always intended as a future botanic garden. It received 3,500,000 tons of **residential and commercial trash**, all from the South Bay area, from 1957 to 1965, a total of 1,150,000 vehicle loads. As soon as each section of the planned garden was full, development was initiated.

The **first plantings** of over 40,000 donated plants were done in 1961, and the buildings constructed in 1963 and '64. A non-profit foundation was established to coordinate the enthusiastic community support for the garden project. One unexpected difficulty with the early development of the garden was the negative effect the heat generated by the decomposing garbage had on the roots of new plants.

The second part of the landfill, called the **Mainland Fill Site**, was across the street from the Botanic Garden, between Crenshaw and Hawthorne Boulevards. It was in use from 1961 to 1980 and took in 18,300,000 tons of waste material. This was for the most part household and commercial waste, but 4% was Class I (the least dangerous) hazardous material, mostly drilling mud and refinery waste.

The third part was where **Ernie Howlett Park** now stands, on the west side of Hawthorne Boulevard. It took in 1,800,000 tons of mostly construction and demolition waste.

Today the Mainland and Botanic Garden sites are owned by L.A. County, while Ernie Howlett Park is owned by the city of Rolling Hills Estates. The Sanitation District continues to monitor the **environmental status** of all three, with a system of some 250 probes, made of perforated pipe, that measure the gas content in the refuse. In 1985 a small area of groundwater contamination was discovered in the Mainland site, and a subsurface barrier of clay and cement was constructed to contain it. Wells to extract liquid were put in behind the barrier and in the near future 27 additional wells will be put in to reduce the likelihood of another incident. The treated water from these wells goes into the sewer system.

One of the most innovative projects in the country in

Pipes cross the Mainland Landfill.

waste technology is also underway at the landfill. Gas wells scattered through the Mainland and Garden sites are all connected to a header pipeline. A vacuum system sends 10% of the gas (which is a methane-CO_2-oxygen mix with a dash of trace elements like Sulfur to give it an interesting aroma) through a gas turbine. The remaining gas gets burned off. The generation system, located in the red brick building across from the Garden drive, produces one megawatt of electricity per year, enough to service 2,000 homes.

On the other side of the Mainland site (on Hawthorne Boulevard) a new **gas energy plant** is now operating. It utilizes much more of the gas in a more cost-effective facility, using the gas to heat boilers in a steam-driven turbine system. This produces 12-13 megawatts of electricity, enough to service 20-25,000 homes. The power is sold to Edison and the money used for site maintenance.

The pipes that spider across the landfill have been laid out for a future 18-hole golf course, to be developed when economic conditions are right and when the quantities of gasses produced have lessened.

MILEAGE **Return to Crenshaw Boulevard and turn left, con-**
   0   **tinuing to the top of the hill.**

	MILEAGE
You will notice that the Botanic Garden driveway and sections of Crenshaw below Palos Verdes Drive North are in bad shape due to **differential settling** of the landfill material.	.1
On your right you will pass the Recycling Center and Rolling Hills Estates **City Hall** (on what was the site of the Thorsen Ranch).	.2
Cross Palos Verdes Drive North.	.3
On your right is the building that houses the Palos Verdes Peninsula News, the newspaper that has served the area for fifty years. The first publication on the Peninsula was the **Palos Verdes Bulletin**, first published in 1925 to distribute information about the Project to prospective clients. It was filled with local news, remarkable photographs, and advertisements touting the benefits of the Palos Verdes area. A lack of funds caused the demise of the Bulletin in 1933.	.4

In 1937 a Yugoslavian immigrant named **John J. Knezevich**, enthusiastic about his new home in Palos Verdes, started the Palos Verdes News, with a masthead reading "American Living At Its Finest". Knezevich made his small paper nationally respected with his new analysis and editorials. While he was away serving in the U.S. Army during World War II, his wife took over the editorial job and kept the paper going, and after his return the paper continued to prosper until his retirement in 1958.

After several changes of ownership, the paper was sold in 1966 to F.F. Stannard, an Ohio attorney and publisher, and his conservative outlook guided the paper through the sixties and seventies. It was renamed the **Palos Verdes Peninsula News** in 1973, and was purchased by, Baker Communications, owner of several southern California newspapers, in 1986.

On the hilltop to the right is the **Chadwick School**,	.6

Botanic Garden

one of California's oldest and most prestigious private schools. It was founded in 1936 by Commander and Mrs. Joseph Chadwick, on 35 acres of land donated by the Palos Verdes Corporation. A few years later they purchased an additional 70 acres for $150 per acre. The school has been attended by many famous people including Liza Minnelli and the children of President Reagan, Joan Crawford, Jack Benny, Van Johnson and George Burns.

1.2   As you drive up the hill through **Agua Negra Canyon,** you will see pipes sticking out of the rock walls, put in to drain water from the rock and minimize weathering. The walls are covered with a fairly good example of coastal sage scrub habitat. In the spring the purple sages give the slopes a violet tinge, and in the fall delicate stephanomaria line the roadside.

1.6   **Continue on Crenshaw Boulevard past Silver Spur and Indian Peak Roads.**

2.1   On the corner of Crenshaw and Crestridge Road stands the **Palos Verdes Art Center**. The organization was founded in 1931 and is supported by the community. It holds exhibitions by local artists, provides services for member artists and offers classes in the arts and related fields.

2.4   **Continue through the four-way stop at Crest Road.**

To the left on Crest Road was the campus of **Palos Verdes College**, a junior college that opened in 1947. Occupying prefabricated buildings left over from the war, the college welcomed students from all over the country and was recognized for its academic excellence. Financial difficulties led to its closing in 1951, but many faculty members remained on the Peninsula. The buildings were taken over by the School District and eventually replaced by a housing development.

2.9   **Turn right on Park Place into Del Cerro Park.**

◆Stop 12.

Del Cerro Park

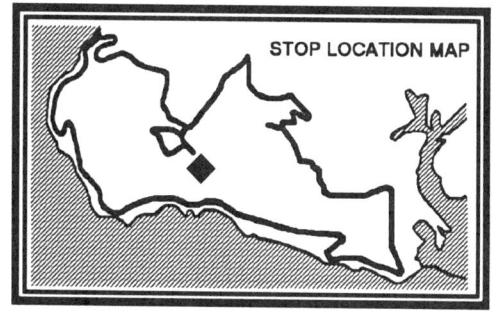

Park in the lot and walk to the top of the hill for a magnificent view of the southern side of the Peninsula. This 6.3-acre park was created in 1983 with the assistance of the Burrell family, who developed the Park Place tract surrounding the park. It was named "**Del Cerro**" or "of the hilltop" after a contest run by the city to select and appropriate name. It is the only legal place to fly radio-controlled planes in Rancho Palos Verdes; all flyers must belong to the Silent Flyers Club and be licensed by the city of Rancho Palos Verdes.

From the top of the rise you can see the **coastline** from Point Vicente to the Portuguese Bend area. The two points below you are Portuguese Point, on the right, and Inspiration Point, and the half circle between them is called variously Sacred Cove, Harden Cove, or Smugglers Cove.

You are also looking down upon the **landslide** areas. Directly below you is the Abalone Cove landslide. On the east side of Inspiration Point is the largest slide, known as the Portuguese Bend slide, covering the entire hollowed out area behind the beach at Portuguese Bend. Further to the left and high on the hillside is the "Flying Triangle" area, named for a brand and now having problems with sliding due to poor water drainage. You can also see clearly the route that Crenshaw Boulevard would have taken if it had been completed, now just a dirt road winding down the hillside.

If you look closely among the trees half-way down and to the right you will see a small Greek temple and, some way below it, a large building with a tile roof, surrounded by trees. These are part of the original **Vanderlip Estate**, built by the man who had the first grand vision of what the Peninsula could become.

In 1913 George Bixby decided to give up cattle ranching and sell the 16,000 acres of **Rancho de los Palos Verdes**. His first buyer, a man named Walter Fundenburg, had trouble financing the agreed-upon purchase price of $1,500,000. He was, however, able to interest Frank A. Vanderlip, then president of the National City Bank of New York, in the property and he put together a syndicate to purchase and develop the Peninsula.

Their **plans** were always **grandiose**. The syndicate hired architects Myron Hunt of Los Angeles and Howard Shaw of Chicago, and the famous landscape engineering company of Frederick Law Olmstead to submit designs for the development. A country club with 150 guest rooms and numerous dining and community rooms was to be built on the cliffs overlooking Portuguese Bend. When the U.S. entered World War I, however, the members of the syndicate had little time for west-coast developments and the project was abandoned.

Frank Vanderlip remained interested, nonetheless, and his involvement in the Palos Verdes project was to last for decades. His was a true American rags to riches tale - born in Illinois on a farm, he taught himself stenography and was hired by the local newspaper. He studied finance at the Universities of Illinois and Chicago and was chosen as the Financial Editor of the *Chicago Tribune* and then as an Assistant Secretary of the Treasury under McKinley. In 1901 he resigned from government to go into banking, and by 1909 was President of National City Bank in New York. One year later, at the age of 46, he was a millionaire.

In order to choose the best possible spot for his own home, Vanderlip commissioned Dr. Ford Ashman Carpenter, a former head of the U.S. Weather Bureau office in Los Angeles, to complete a **weather survey** of the Peninsula. He recommended an elevation of 500 feet above Abalone Cove as having the nearly perfect climate - much sunshine, little fog, light winds, not too much humidity, and a pleasant range of temperatures.

Although the **Vanderlip** family still spent most of their time at their New York estate, called Beechwood, in 1916 they began building a **summer home** on the site they had chosen. Materials and furnishings had to be brought in from San Pedro on a difficult dirt road. Frank, his wife Narcissa Cox Vanderlip (a noted suffragette and philanthropist), and their six children spent vacations for many years at the "Old Ranch Cottage". Visitors were numerous and Sunday lunches included interesting people from all over the area.

Lucky Baldwin, a mining prospector and developer, was a frequent visitor. Claiming that the place was too quiet, he brought in a flock of **peacocks**. Later other birds were added until the collection held over 500 varieties, with four acres of cages. It was the responsibility of the young Vanderlip children to feed and care for the birds. Eventually all but the peacocks were given to the Wrigley estate on Catalina Island. Today descendants of those original peacocks roam the streets in Portuguese Bend, Rolling Hills, Margate and other neighborhoods, filling the air with their harsh cries.

Peninsula residents have mixed feelings about the peafowl. Although they are beautiful creatures and add an interesting aspect to residential areas, they can **damage** roofs, gardens and automobiles. Rolling Hills Estates brought in a peafowl expert in 1992 who successfully advised residents how to coexist peacefully with their feathered neighbors.

Additional buildings were constructed by the Vanderlips during the next decade, intended eventually to surround their **mansion**, which was to be a copy of an Italian villa built by Pope Julius III and was to be built on on of the knolls below you to the right. In the early 1920's, guest houses called "La Casetta", and the "Villetta" were built, along with a barn and stables later to become the Riding Club (just visible from Del Cerro halfway between the ocean and the open space). From the Villetta a flight of 268 marble steps rose to a lookout point and the white marble temple you see from above. Seeds for the cypress trees that lined the staircases were brought from the Bogoli gardens in Rome, but most of the trees were burned in a fire many years later. A horseshoe-shaped road with gatehouses was built from what is now Palos Verdes Drive South to provide access to the Vanderlip estate.

In 1925 Vanderlip commissioned the famous French model maker, Jacques Greber, to build **detailed models** of his mansion and the artisans village he planned for Point Vicente. These large (5' by 6' and 8' x 6'), beautifully-detailed models were brought to the Peninsula in 1978 by the Rancho de los Palos Verdes Historical Society. In 1928 marble was imported from Italy to begin construction of the mansion and grading was done but when the stock market crashed in 1929 the plans were abandoned.

Several others joined the Vanderlips during the 20's. Harry Benedict had been hired by Frank Vanderlip as a trainee in his bank. From that lowly beginning he went on to become involved in the finances of the Palos Verdes Corporation, join the Board of Directors of Barker Brothers Furniture Co., and help organize American Airlines. His home, called **Villa Francesca** after his wife, occupies an 11-acre site across from Portuguese Point. It has been commemorated by a plaque installed by the Historical Society.

Edward Harden, President of the Colgate & Co. Bank of New York, was married to Mrs. Vanderlip's sister. He chose the land at **Portuguese Point** and had gardens designed and laid out by the Olmstead Brothers. A tower based on one in Ospilaletto, Italy (designed by the famous architect Pallado in the 16th century) was built to mark the entrance to the estate. It was built on a single foundation so that it would give in one piece if the earth were to move (did he have a crystal ball?). A mansion with 50 bedrooms was planned for the crest of the point, but was never built because of the Depression. All that remained was a summer house, pergola and gardens and even those have largely disappeared today.

The point and the cove have been the setting for many **movies** and TV shows, notably "*It's a Mad, Mad, Mad, Mad World*" in 1963, "*Winds of War*", *The Thorn Birds*", "*Perry Mason*", "*The War Lords*", "*The Other Side of Midnight*", "*Remington Steele,*" "*Twins,*" and "*Lethal Weapon*".

The tall (up to 8'), lacy green plant that grows on the hillside is **sweet fennel,** or anise. The leaves have feathery filaments that smell like licorice when crushed. Heads of tiny

yellow flowers in spring and summer are followed by licorice-scented seeds, up to 750 per stem in attractive clusters.

This Mediterrean plant, though pretty and sweet-smelling, is seen as a real **nuisance on the Peninsula** by those interested in preservation of native plants and habitat. With its huge numbers of seeds, drought-tolerance, and toughness, it crowds out the more fragile native plants.

Another common plant is **wild mustard,** tall and thin with lobed leaves, hairy stems, and small yellow flowers. One variety blooms all at once in late spring, covering the hillsides with yellow, while the other has flowers that last from spring until winter. Both the leaves and the seeds (in flat pods) taste like mustard and are edible. Legend has it that the Spanish missionaries sowed the plant as they struggled along the overland trails from Mexico. When they were ready to return, aisles of yellow-flowered bushes marked their path.

MILEAGE

0   **Leave the parking lot and turn left onto Crenshaw Boulevard.**

.4   **Turn left at the four-way stop onto Crest Road, and then take your third right onto Highridge**
1.0   **Road.**

1.7   **At the second stop sign turn right onto Crestridge Road.**

1.9   The land on the west side of Highridge Road across

from Crestridge was the site of the **Wallace "antenna farm"**. In 1939 Kelvin Vanderlip sold 129 acres of land on the very top of the Peninsula to Press Wireless, a group of 12 newspapers, who used it to contact news sources in the South Pacific.

In 1949 **Don Wallace**, who had been heavily involved in the communications for the Treaty of Versailles and Radio Officer for the Presidential yacht, bought the land and sold all but 24 acres, retaining most of the antennas. Over the next decades, his call letters "W6AM" became famous throughout the world and he was known for his ability to reach other countries even before commercial antennas could. Wallace died in 1985, leaving more than 20,000 documents and rooms full of awards. His 61 poles were a notable local sight and will be commemorated in a museum on part of the site, which has been developed with luxury homes.

Crestridge Road is sometimes called "Church Street" because it is lined with churches. There were several early ranches belonging to the McCarrell family in this area. During World War II, the land where the Congregation Ner Tamid Synagogue now stands was site of the **communication center** for southern California, providing information for an area of more than 4,000 square miles. It had walls of 12-inch thick, steel-reinforced concrete, painted with doors and windows so that from the air it looked like an ordinary warehouse. Its poison-gas-proof entrance led to a room filled with communications equipment able to notify citizens of an enemy raid in two and one-half minutes.

MILEAGE

2.0

Turn left on Crenshaw at the light. 2.2

Go one block to the light and turn left on Indian Peak Road. Almost immediately turn right into the parking lot of the small office complex. Park in the first spot available on your left. Walk back up to the sidewalk overlooking the valley. 2.3

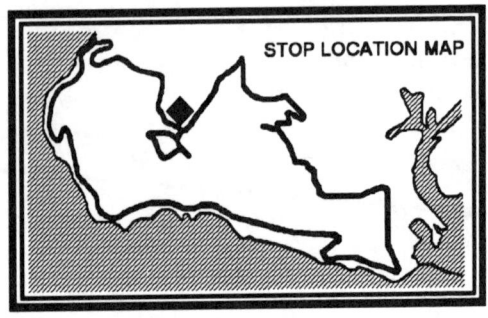

◆ **Stop 13.**

Indian Peak Overlook

From this overlook you can see the major shopping district of the Peninsula. From the very beginning Palos Verdes was planned as a largely residential community. Recognizing the need for a convenient source of groceries, goods and supplies, however, the early planners set aside discrete areas for commerce. There are those who feel that even this much **commercial development** is antithetic to the nature of Peninsula life, but most feel that the convenience it provides makes their lives easier.

This deep depression was called **Long Valley** when the early sheepherders used it as a camping site, and later was known as Deep Valley. Some say that this area was known as "skunk hollow," but others feel that that name refers to part of the Palos Verdes Golf Course. At any rate, this area was generally very damp. A spring flowed near the junction of Silver Spur and Crenshaw, and during wet years the valley at times filled with water, forming a lake drained by rivers through the canyons now occupied by Hawthorne and Crenshaw Boulevards.

Crenshaw Canyon was the largest on the north side of the Peninsula, and was variously called Agua Negra Canyon, after the dark water that came from the spring, or Purple Rock Canyon, after the color of the rocks exposed there. The origin of the Crenshaw name is unknown, but it was given to the street farther north in the city of Los Angeles.

The Talking Flower Clock

During the first part of the century this land formed part of the **ranches** that spread across the center of the Peninsula. A photograph taken in the '30s from Rancho Elastico, on the hillside above the valley, shows a winding road traversing it and piles of hay. Thoroughbred race horses were corralled on the valley floor.

The **undeveloped land** behind you was approved for development as a life-care facility in 1990. The Marriott Corporation plans to build a quarter-mile-long building with apartments, a nursing home, and a hospital. Some local residents challenged the project in court which, along with the faltering economy, has delayed its implementation.

The **towers** on the top of the hill are part of the emergency communication system for the South Bay, providing dishes to transmit messages to rescue vehicles and facilities.

Peninsula Center and the pink building (formerly Buffum's) on the far left were the first stores to be built in the area, in the 1960's, along with the Town & Country Shopping Center on the far right. During the mid-70's a **controversial** proposal by the May Store Shopping Centers to construct an enclosed **mall** in the central section was finally abandoned. The unresolved problems included the proposed shifting of Deep Valley Drive, the sharing of revenues between the two cities involved (Rancho Palos Verdes, which owned Hawthorne and Crenshaw Boulevards, and Rolling Hills Estates, which owned the land to be developed), and potential costs for police and fire protection. It was resolved when Rolling Hills Estates agreed to pay a small portion of the sales tax it collects to Rancho Palos Verdes in return for the curb cuts needed to provide access to the commercial area.

A master plan for the development of the remaining land in the center of the Peninsula was completed by the RHE Planning Commission in 1978. Shortly thereafter developers Ernest Hahn and Ron Florance submitted a plan for the 14 acres of land still vacant. After months of negotiations, the two cities came to an agreement and work began on the **Courtyard Mall**. It was designed by two California firms to hold two major department store (ironically, one was to be the May Co., owned by the company that had first tried to build on the site), 92 specialty shops and restaurants, an ice skating rink and a community meeting room. The mall opened in the fall of 1981 and the theaters were added in 1984.

Later that year a **major fire** began in the theater construction area and spread into the mall. More than three dozen firefighting units from all over the South Bay fought for four hours to control the blaze, which did more than $1 million worth of damage.

In 1990 the mall was sold, and renamed **The Shops at Palos Verdes**. Today it has more than 70 shops and restaurants, including I. Magnin, the May Company, Brentano's Books and the Nature Company, and live and movie theaters.

In 1979 the QBM Project in which you are standing was constructed. The upper level has 25,000 square feet of office space and a restaurant. The lower level, now called **the Brick Walk**, has boutiques and restaurants.

The white building to the right of the Shops at Palos Verdes is the **Peninsula Center Library**, built in 1967. It is the central library for the Palos Verdes Library District and holds more than 200,000 books in a modern facility. Special collections include over 10,000 sound recordings, language tapes, books on tape, video cassettes, large print books and musical scores.

In 1991 local voters (voting more than 70% in favor) approved a **bond measure** to double the size of the library, increase the seating area and collection, reconfigure the parking and generally improve the facility.

	MILEAGE
The road down from this parking lot leads to Deep Valley Drive but it is a private road not intended for through traffic. Return to Indian Peak Road and turn right.	0
Continue to the second light, at Crossfield Road and turn right.	.3
On your left you will pass one of the Los Angeles County **fire stations**. Fire protection on the Peninsula is provided by five stations, run by the County, which also provides paramedic services.	.3
On your right is the **Norris Theater**. This theater is the fulfillment of years of hard work by a Peninsulan, Agnes Moss. In 1978 she formed the Community Association of the Peninsula (CAP) and asked the developers of the Courtyard Mall to help create a local theater. Ernest Hahn and Ron Florance donated the land and money to begin construction. A major contribution from Mr. and Mrs. Kenneth Norris, along with local support, completed the project. The theater is now rarely dark - presenting plays, music, dance and community events. Major stars and productions appear regularly, bringing an exciting extra dimension to Peninsula life.	.4

MILEAGE	
.4	Continue straight through the light at Deep Valley Drive.
.5	On your right you will see the **"Talking Clock"** donated to the city by the Medawar Time Corporation. Covered with flowers and decorated with a waterfall, the clock plays the National Anthem at noon and tells the time each hour. It is the centerpiece of a small landscaped public park.
	Mr. Michel Medawar was a watch repairer in Beruit, Lebanon, who worked for kings in the Middle East, and installed the prayer clocks in the Great Mosque of Mecca. In 1975 he came to Rancho Palos Verdes and opened a jewelry store. Some years later he wanted to express his appreciation to his adopted country, so he designed and organized the placing of the flower clock on land donated by Terry Cole, a local developer. It was **dedicated** in 1987 by local notables and actor Danny Thomas.
.6	Turn left onto Silver Spur Road.
.7	The **Peninsula Center** Shopping area on your left was one of the first on the Peninsula. It has changed hands several times in recent years, and will be undergoing reconstruction in 1993.
.8	Continue across Hawthorne Boulevard.
	On your right you will pass **Palos Verdes Peninsula High School**, designated a California distinguished school in 1991-92, its first year of operation after the the consolidation of three highs schools into one in 1991. Both California Presidential Scholars were from PVPHS in 1992, and the school had more merit scholar finalists than any other California school (and was 12th in the nation). The girls basketball team was rated number one in the country by USA Today, and other sports teams (with their Panther emblem) are nearly all the best in the state or league. The Mathematics team is number one in the nation,

the Latin and Physics teams are the California State MILEAGE Champions, and many other groups are county, state and national winners.

The **Palos Verdes Unified School District** covers 24 square miles and has approximately 8,000 students. It is governed by a Board of Education made up of five elected members who serve for four years. In addition to the high school, there are two intermediate schools, eight elementary schools, and a continuation high school.

In recent years declining enrollments, caused by high home prices, have created funding problems for the school district, but **community involvement** keeps the quality of education extremely high. The private, non-profit Peninsula Education Foundation raises almost a half million dollars per year to benefit the school district.

Just past the school athletic fields, pull over to the right side of the road, next to the tennis courts, where you have a view of the city below. 1.0

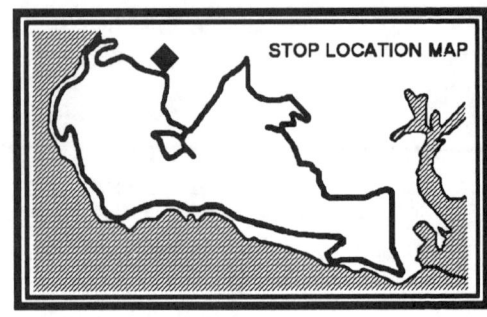

◆ Stop 14.

Silver Spur Road
at Palos Verdes Peninsula High School

From the crest of the hill here you can see (except when the smog's in your way) the city of Los Angeles and several smaller cities spread out before you. At night the city lights are a **magnificent spectacle.**

If you had been standing here on February 25, 1942, you would have had a splendid view of the famous **L.A. air raid.** Searchlights raked the skies for enemy planes. Every gun on the coast fired continuously, filling the air with red blasts. More than 1,477 shells were fired by the anti-aircraft guns, though in the end no trace of Japanese bombs or planes could be found.

From this spot you also may see one of the five **blimps** that soar through the air over the Peninsula, belonging to Goodyear, MetLife, Budweiser, Fuji Film and Virgin Atlantic. The blimp presence here began with the Goodyear's Columbia, which is headquartered in Carson and is one of three identical blimps maintained by the tire company (the others are in Texas and Florida).

The Columbia is 192' long and holds 202,000 cubic feet of helium. The cabin below it can hold six people plus a pilot, or a pilot, cameraperson, videoperson and a complex assortment of TV equipment. On Mondays and Tuesdays the blimp sits on the ground for maintenance but during the rest of the week it travels where it's needed for the overhead camera angle nothing else can provide.

For centuries the northern side of the Peninsula inland from the coast was dry and lifeless for most of the year, and few traces of early habitation have been found. It was not until the 1920's that the area's scenic beauty inspired development in the shape of the very unusual **Palos Verdes Project**.

The Palos Verdes Project was something new and daring in the field of real estate. The concept was originated by promoter **E.G. Lewis**, a hustler and schemer in the grand manner. In his checkered past he had been a candy salesman, had set up a pyramid scheme to sell watches, established the People's University (one of the first correspondence schools) and developed the planned communities of Universal City in St. Louis and Atascadero near San Luis Obispo. Suits for fraud alternated with public acclaim for his latest enterprise.

Lewis was also the founder of **The Commonwealth**, an organization that considered "brains and effort as capital and on exactly the same footing as money." This unique business notion aside, his arrangements for the new real estate venture, the Palos Verdes Project, sounded slightly more businesslike, if very optimistic.

Lewis's plan, introduced to potential investors in 1922, was to sell trust indenture notes (like shares) in the **new city** he planned to create on land to be purchased from Mr. Vanderlip. His official proposals estimated the costs at $5 million for the land and $30 million for parks, schools, public buildings, clubs, golf links, flying fields, a yacht harbor, and roads, all to be built in three years. There were two sorts of notes - "convertible" ones that entitled the purchaser to select land of a value equal to the investment, and "nonconvertible" ones that entitled the purchaser to a share of any profits. No construction would begin until $15 million worth of notes had been purchased.

All preliminary **costs of the project** were to be born by Lewis, who estimated their amount at $250,000 (though they quickly reached $750,000). Lewis then turned around and asked for personal loans from members of the Commonwealth to cover the costs.

Thousands of people did subscribe to the venture, perhaps swayed by Lewis's assurances that "your decision to subscribe may mean much more to you than any investment you have ever made or are likely ever to make." A photograph from the time shows a capacity crowd of 4229 of the Underwriters meeting at the Los Angeles Philharmonic Auditorium. Based on this **early success**, the landscape firm of the Olmstead Brothers was hired to supervise the layout of the project, and other experts in the fairly new field of city planning joined enthusiastically in the venture.

Then suddenly things fell apart. The financial organization overseeing the Project declared that all the required conditions had not been met, that the trust was being dissolved, and that monies would be refunded. Frank Vanderlip quickly came from New York to **save the project**. A new organization, called the Commonwealth Trust Company, was set up to continue the work on a smaller scale. The one million dollars that remained was used to buy 3200 acres of land in the areas that are now Miraleste and Palos Verdes Estates. Within a few months the new enterprise was back on track.

As was his way, a few months later Lewis left the Trust for newer and greener pastures. (He eventually went to jail for unrelated fraud.) New financial managers took over but the same group of **far-seeing planners** who had worked from the beginning to design the new community remained in charge of the Project: the Olmsteads, Frank Vanderlip, and Charles H. Cheney (sometimes called Harry), a noted city planner and architect who was also involved in the design of Rolling Hills. It was Cheney who drew up the **master plan** and wrote the basic restrictions that are still valid for Palos Verdes Estates. A Homes Association and Art Jury were set up to enforce the regulations. All construction had to be designed by an architect, be of an appropriate value, and be pleasing to the eye. Roofs were uniform in each area, either clay tile or cedar shake, and paint colors had to conform to the prevailing light tones. Other regulations governed details like the set-backs, the siting of trash cans, and the percentage of lot coverage. The plan was put into effect for 37 years, with automatic extension for periods of 20 years unless two-thirds of the property owners voted to change it.

Ninety percent of the lots in the new community were restricted to **one-family homes**. Six commercial areas were allowed - at Malaga Cove, Lunada Bay, Valmonte, Margate, Montemalaga and Miraleste. Half of the area was reserved for parks and roadways. The restrictions also provided that *There shall not be any saloon, foundry, brick-yard, cemetery, slaughter-house, tannery, oil refinery or fish cannery in the town.* The keeping of animals and poultry, except dogs and cats, was prohibited.

In many ways the early days of the Palos Verdes Project were a **grand experiment**, one that received international attention. Journals in Quebec, Berlin and London mentioned the new endeavor as an example of what could be done in the field of city planning.

By the mid-1920's houses began to appear on the landscape, some built by the planners themselves. An enormous **real estate campaign** began, luring thousands to the Peninsula as potential investors. On Sundays free lunches and entertainment brought up to 800 visitors in one afternoon. The Palos Verdes Bulletin, providing news of the Project and ads for the venture, was mailed to people all over the world.

Real estate **brochures** were also available, praising the project in fulsome terms: "The *City Beautiful* has long been a dream of humanity. But at last the dream has come true, every detail perfectly created ..."

Straight ahead of you down the hill lies the neighborhood of

Valmonte, one of the first on the Peninsula. On Via Valmonte, off Palos Verdes Drive North, is the Tower House, also called the Via Mirlo Gate Lodge, a two-story, stone structure 15 feet in diameter. Constructed in 1925, it marked the main entrance to the Project from Los Angeles. Extensive plantings around the entrance turned it into a blaze of color.

The Olmsteads set up a **nursery** in Lunada Bay to make plants available to residents at cost, along with advice about gardening (necessary for those trying to landscape a desert). By 1928 a memo noted that coastal redwoods, live oaks, 10 varieties of eucalyptus, 5 types of pines and 3 types of cypress had been planted, for a total of 11,000 trees. Twenty-five miles of street trees were planted, along with native trees and shrubs suited to slopes, and decorative trees comfortable on windswept bluffss. In all, several hundred thousand plants added their greenery to the slopes of the once barren Peninsula.

MILEAGE

0   Continue down Silver Spur Road. Turn left after
.4   .4 mile (at the light) onto Montemalaga Road.

.7   The canyon that cuts deep into the hillside is Malaga Canyon, the largest on the north side of the Peninsula. At the base of the hill it swings around to the west and eventually empties into Malaga Cove.

1.1   Past the canyon on your right you will see a promontory of empty land. This is called **Grandview Park** and was to have been the site of a Junior High School. It was purchased by the City of Rancho Palos Verdes for $175,000 and may some day be a developed park. The Grandview tract, surrounding it, one of the oldest developments on the Peninsula.

Below you on the hillside (just out of sight) is the **Palos Verdes Country Club**. Its first building was opened in 1924, followed by more construction in the succeeding years. The 213-acre course with grass greens and fairways was highly rated and considered difficult. The golf team competed nationally, and the course hosted the Palos Verdes Open beginning in 1928. Douglas Fairbanks, Sr. caused a stir when he attended the Open as a spectator in the '30s. In later years Bing Crosby and Johnny Weismuller played in the Invitational Tournament at the Club. The dry conditions on the Peninsula kept the greens very hard, and the course was famous for long balls. In recent years several nationally-ranked players have come from the Club.

MILEAGE

You will cross from Rancho Palos Verdes into Palos Verdes Estates. Turn right onto Via del Monte.   **1.2**
  1.4

Over to your left near the intersection of Vias Visalia and Mirabel stood the **barracks** that housed the soldiers manning the observation stations during World War II.

This street was one of the first on the Peninsula and it holds some of the **oldest houses**. Just after the first stop sign you will pass #881 on your left, designed by architect Kirtland Cutter for the Cameron family and built in 1924 for $25,000. The Palos Verdes Art Jury chose it as the Best House of 1924.   **1.8**

Pull over to the right side of the road, where Via del Sol joins Via del Monte at an angle. You will be more-or-less across from Via Coches.   **2.0**

Silver Spur

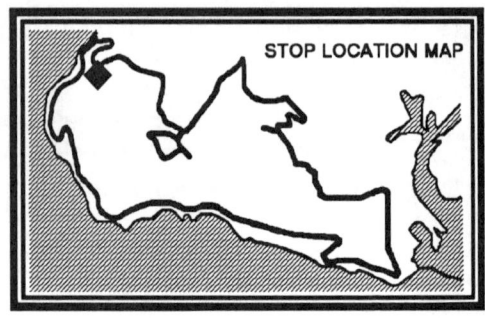

STOP LOCATION MAP

◆Stop 15.

La Venta Inn

The **towered building** below you and to the left is one of the oldest on the Peninsula. For many years it stood alone on the hillside, its rooms and terrances offering a spectacular view of the coastline from Malibu to Bluff Cove.

When it was built for $17,000 in 1923, the Inn was first called "Clubhouse 764". The name was soon changed to **La Venta**, "the sale", because it was the place where potential customers were brought to sign up for a piece of Palos Verdes. After a dining room was added for $8,250 in 1924, clients were given lunch or dinner and then taken to a cottage outside that served as a closing office for making deals.

The building was designed by Pierpont and Walter Davis as a model for the type of house desired in the Palos Verdes Project, and it was chosen in 1929 as one of the "Ten Most **Notable Buildings** in Palos Verdes". Rare and exotic plants were grown in the courtyard to demonstrate the possibilities for landscaping and to test new varities for their suitability.

Local sightseers and visitors from other states and countries began coming to La Venta for meals and overnight stays, though only a few rooms were available. Among the stars making a stay at the Inn during its **celebrity years** were Charles Lindbergh, Erroll Flynn, Betty Grable, Bob Hope, Fred MacMurray, Merle Oberon, Hedy LaMarr, Lana Turner and Robert Stack. It was also the setting for several movies, including *Spanish Sunlight*, a film starring Barbara LaMarr and Lewis Stone in 1925.

The Inn was primarily an elegant place for local residents to dine and celebrate. The first **wedding** was held on the terrace in 1925. Meals were reasonably priced - in 1925 breakfast cost $1.00, luncheon was $1.50, tea was $.50 and dinner was $2.00!

The Inn managed to scrape through the Depression and then nearly went out of business during World War II due to blackouts, shortages and rationing. For a short time the tower was used as an **observation station**. Finally, in 1945, it was sold to Commander Schnetzler, a retired naval officer, and his wife, who used it as their home.

In 1954 the Inn was reopened by Robert and Del Eskridge, who were featured in a 1987 PEOPLE Magazine article as they renewed their wedding vows in the courtyard of the Inn. Today the Sepulveda family flag still hangs in the living room, and the gardens have been redone to restore them to the spirit of the innovative early designs.

MILEAGE

Continue down Via del Monte.   **0**

On your left, just past Via Coches, is house #833,   **.05**

MILEAGE **Villa Del Mare**, with its lion gateposts and large, arched picture window. It was designed by J.C. Koppel and built in 1931 by Patrick and Lenora Lizza. Undoubtedly due to the Depression, the house cost only $8,000, two thousand less than required, but an asterisk on the building permit notes that the minimum amount required for the lot was reduced by resolution.

.2 On your right you will pass the **entrance** to the La Venta Inn. The parking lot is private and is often open only to those attending weddings or other functions at the Inn.

> Many more houses on this street were built during the earliest days of the project. If you are a student of **architectural history**, you may want to pull over and locate these houses, **but it's not safe to try to spot them as you drive**. If you're not interested in houses from the '20s and '30s, skip the indented section.

.6 *House #**744**, a two-story house with an indented balcony and green trim, was built in 1928 by J.R. Peterson for $20,000.

*House #**740**, with a magenta awning and an ivy-covered lawn, was built in 1926 for $9,000 by J.H. Gaines.

.7 *House #**720**, built in 1931, is a stepped back house with blue trim and an olive tree in the front yard. Mrs. Elizabeth W. Albee had it built for $12,000.

*The house at #**712** was another award winner, chosen as the "**Most Notable House of 1929**" by the Art Jury. It was built in 1928 by Walter J. Braunsweiger, Vice President of the Bank of Italy (which at that point was one of the Project's trustees), for $13,800. It has a tile-framed picture window and a wrought-iron balcony.

*House **#640**, with its inset tile picture, stucco garage and rocky yard, was also built in 1924, by Messrs. Roe and Roetner for $10,000.

MILEAGE
.8

*A stone staircase leads to house **#632**, which is decorated with wrought-iron balconies. It was built in 1930 for $10,000 by Clarence Lee, who was active in the community.

*The charming tall house with the glass-walled room at **#624** was built in 1925 by Carl M. Sebelius, whose wife was later a founder of the first Sunday school.

.9

*On the ocean side of the street, house **#613**, with its quarter-circle balcony lined with ornate wooden spokes, was built in 1926 by Miss Mary M. Cain.

*House **#605** was also a ladies' residence, built in 1931 for Blanche R. Randall and Cora R. Conklin.

*For **#577**, a small peach stucco house, Joseph E. Callaway listed himself and Hamilton as the architects in 1925.

*House **#548**, of white brick, received building permit #16 in 1924. It was built for the Palos Verdes Project by J.C. Rous at a cost of $14,000.

*Dr. Ulric B. Bray, a consultant in petroleum and industrial chemistry and later a City Councilman, built the house at **#541** in 1930 for $7,900.

All drivers, however, can look (at .8 mile) for #657 Via del Monte, "La Casa de la Curva", which sits behind a fern-lined wall. This was the **home of Charles H. Cheney**, the city planner who wrote the Project's architectural regulations, and his wife Cora who was the first president of the Palos Verdes Women's Club. Many years later, Mrs. Cheney, who continued to be very active in civic affairs, wrote a letter to the local newspaper apologizing for the fact that her

(.8)

MILEAGE family's laundry was visible from the road (a fact that she had just discovered) and asking all residents to eliminate the eyesore of visible laundry from the Palos Verdes hillsides. The house was designed by Walter and Windell Davis and built in 1924 for $18,500.

1.25 At 1.25 miles, at the bottom of the hill just after the stop sign at Via Corta, pull over to the right in front of Farnham Martin Park. You will see a stone wall with a lawn and fountain behind it.

Farnham B. Martin was Superintendent of Parks for the Palos Verdes Project until he was tragically killed in an automobile accident in 1928. The newly finished park was dedicated to the man who had designed many of the gardens in the Project and supervised their installation and maintenance. Its landscaping and bubbling fountain cost the Homes Association $9,500. In later years the park was used as a site for scout meetings, and in 1934 for a Camp Fire Girls Carnival. Concerts and weddings are still held on the oval lawn.

Construction was also begun on the building beside the park, the **Malage Cove Library**, in 1928. It was designed by Myron Hunt, under the direction of a library board that included Romayne Martin (Farnham's widow) and Charles Cheney, to serve both as a library and art gallery. A local woodcarver named Meredith Watts made replicas of antique Renaissance period tables and chairs provided by the Vanderlips.

After a successful bond issue that raised $60,000 for its construction, the **new library** was opened in June of 1930. A gilt-edged triptych showing saints ornamented the reading room. Massive beams were exposed in the ceilings. Fresh flowers were provided by the garden club. The librarian, Miss McMillan, would personally select books for young patrons, who would curl up on the leather couches to enjoy an afternoon's read.

The **Exhibit Hall** on the lower floor was the scene for lectures and shows by local artists. Ralph Holmes, a member of the Art Jury, exhibited his landscapes, the California Watercolor Society showed work by 75 of its members, and the Vanderlips lent a collection of rare Pompeian pottery. A Friends of Art Fund, established in 1926, bought the winning entry in the Purchase Prize Exhibit for $500. During the 1930's the Women's Club presented regular lectures in the Gallery, on economic and social issues. In 1933, however, the minutes of the club assured members that the talks would be for "recreation rather than problem talks".

The library was remodeled in 1956 and again in 1963 to hold more than 30,000 books and periodicals, and now has a modern computer system. It is also the site for the **Local History Room** which contains vital documents about peninsula history, including newspaper files, scrapbooks, photographs, tape recordings and yearbooks.

Turn left onto Via Chico and drive through the arch into the Malaga Cove Plaza. Turn left and park.

1.3

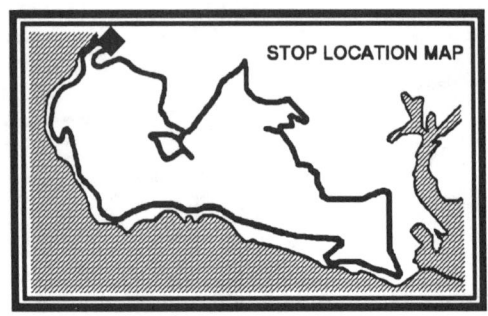

◆**Stop 16**

Malaga Cove Plaza

As you stand in this beautiful plaza you may feel as if you are in a **corner of Europe**. That is precisely what the developers of the Palos Verdes Project wanted you to feel, for they hoped to give the new community an atmosphere of Mediterranean graciousness and charm.

If you are facing the center of the plaza, the farthest forward building on your right is the **Gardner Building**, the first commercial center for the Peninsula, dedicated in 1925 with great fanfare. Many saw the new plaza as a mark of success, and, with the opening of the first post office, a recognition of the community's new, official status.

The **building** was designed by Weber, Staunton and Spaulding, Architects, and cost $57,000 to construct. The entire second floor was taken over by offices for the Engineering and Design Departments of the Palos Verdes Project, the Homes Association, and the Art Jury, all of whom were delighted to move from their old offices in the Redondo Beach Hotel to something closer and more convenient. The ground floor had a grocery store, post office and an office for the sales force for the Project (until La Venta was finished).

The building was described as **Spanish Renaissance style,** with a roof of hand-made Mexican tile burned a deep orange brown. On the front side there are ten arches and on the plaza side four arches, each one overlooked by a small wooden balcony. The arches open onto a pedestrian arcade, and legend has it that, in the European manner, the arcades are designed to be tall enough to allow a knight in full armor on horseback to ride underneath.

Residents were urged to support the **new businesses**, and were pleased to welcome the Bruce Drug Store in 1927 and Moore's Market (still in business today) in 1932. Local students spent the winter of 1928 attending elementary school in the Gardner building until their school was completed the next spring, and it also held the first library, open Tuesdays and Thursdays in the afternoon.

The Art Jury chose the Gardner Building as one of the "Ten Most Notable Buildings in Palos Verdes" in 1929. The original drug store is now replaced by the offices of Merrill Lynch Realty, and the **flower stand**, which has been used in many advertising campaigns, still lends a touch of elegance. In 1980 the building was sold to Hiro Nomura of Japan for $900,000.

The second building in the plaza was the large one on your left, built of weathered brick with turquoise shutters. It was called the **Casa del Portal,** or the Syndicate Building, and includes the arch over Via Chico. Many community organizations called it home over the years, from the Palos Verdes Play School in the late 20's to the Red Cross volunteer and work center in the 40's.

The crowning glory of the plaza is, of course, the famous **Neptune Fountain** in its center. An international art collector named Adolfo di Segni was so taken by the "Gem of the Pacific" coast that he presented the fountain to the community, considering the figure of Neptune to be an appropriate symbol for a city by the sea. He had found the fountain in the courtyard of an old villa north of Venice. It was a two-thirds size copy of a famous bronze fountain in Bologna, Italy, done by Gian Bologna and Palermito Lauretti and erected in 1563. The Palos Verdes Project paid the costs of the statue as a gift to the community.

The life-size god holds a trident and rests his foot on a dolphin. The supporting pedestals are ornamented with **cupids, seahorses, mermaids and genii**. When local ladies objected to the fact that the mermaids squirted water from their breasts, City Planner Cheney reputedly said "But, ladies, we couldn't afford milk!".

The dedication of the fountain, in 1930, was a grand celebration, welcoming the Lt. Governor, famous architects and figures in the art world, and all the residents for miles around. The fountain graced the plaza until 1968 when it had deteriorated so much that it had to be removed. A **new**, slightly smaller **version** carved from Carrera marble, was ordered from Italy, exactly the same as the original statue except for the addition of a modest fig leaf.

Through the years the statue has been the object of repeated **vandalism**. On Halloween it was often dressed in costume, or, in an act that caused severe damage to the sculpture, covered with paint. Thieves have occasionally removed the cherubs and the trident. Molds have been made of both so they can be replaced, but the cost of either is close to $1,000 (not counting installation time and labor).

Today the Malaga Cove **Plaza** houses offices, shops and

numerous realtors, all watched over by the benevolent gaze of Neptune, god of the sea. On weekends, local artist often display their wares on the green lawn fronting the plaza.

Exit the plaza on Via Tejon, in front of the Gardner Building. Turn right on Via Corta and cross Palos Verdes Drive West.

MILEAGE
0

On the opposite corner of Palos Verdes Drive West is the **Palos Verdes Memorial Garden**, a small park dedicated to the three young men (Morris Shipley, John Bleecker and Hammond Dendy Sadler) who lost their lives in World War II. It was designed by Hammond Sadler, Sr., in memory of his son Dendy who in 1944 went down with his plane somewhere in the Pacific Ocean. The park has a pedestal, brass plaques and two stone benches.

.2

Continue down Via Corta. When it bends to the left it becomes Via Almar. After the bend, pull over to the side of the road, where you have a view of the canyon.

.35

To your right is **Malaga Canyon**, one of the major water drainage channels on the Peninsula, collecting water from the northern slopes. It forms an important natural wetland habitat for Peninsula wild-

.35 life. On the far side of the canyon is the **Olmstead Estate**, the home of Frederick Law Olmstead, Jr. His house, on Rosita Place, was the first built directly on the top of the bluffs. Behind it is the St. Francis Episcopal Church.

In March 1933, the **Long Beach earthquake** shook the Peninsula and the rear balcony of the Olmstead House (owned at that time by an English family named Young) fell into the ocean. Other damage on the Peninsula was minor, though more than 50 were killed in Long Beach where the quake was centered. Although the hard rock basement of the Peninsula makes it unlikely that an earthquake will ever do much harm, newspapers all over the country reported that the cliffs of Palos Verdes had slid into the sea, much to the dismay of relatives unaware of the true situation.

Across the ravine you can see a thick stand of **eucalyptus trees**. These were planted by Harry Phillips at the beginning of the century along a wide band across the northern edge of the Peninsula. Supposedly, he planned to use the wood for railroad ties as was done in Australia, but found that they grew more quickly here and that the wood was not straight or dense enough.

.4 Straight ahead you can see a pale building with a tall tower. That is the **Malaga Cove School**, another of the early buildings of the Palos Verdes Project. Once the office building, inn and golf club were completed, the next priority for the planners was the education of their children. Dissatisfied with the schools in Redondo Beach and unhappy with having their children commute so far, the early residents decided to form their own school district. In 1925 the first school board was elected and bonds in the amount of $85,000 were voted. The fact that education was important to them is evidenced by the fact that 82% of the residents voted in the election and they gave the bonds a 100% yes vote.

In April of 1926 the new building, topped with a fantastically crowned **tower** and containing three classrooms, a kindergarten, a principal's office and an auditorium, was opened for a grand total of 35 students. There were three teachers, including Mrs. Edith Perry, who was also the principal. Each student had his or her own movable table painted a bright color. The Woman's Club and school mothers started a cafeteria. The children raised money for a school library, and the Vanderlips donated several 17th century Flemish tapestries to hang in the auditorium.

MILEAGE
.45

MILEAGE The **quality of the education** at the new school was very high. In fact, fifty-four applications were made in the summer of 1927 for students outside the district to attend the school but they were not accepted. The students presented plays, took field trips, entered an annual birdhouse-building competition, planted trees, and built a goldfish pond. After Boyd Comstock, one of the Board members, was chosen as the track and field coach for the Olympics, he hired several of the Olympic competitors as janitors in the school. This helped support the athletes and provided top-notch coaching for the local boys.

The school grew slowly, graduating 14 students in 1930. Children of the Japanese farmers formed part of the school community for years, but when the **local Japanese** were forced to leave in 1942, fifty of the school's children sadly departed with their families. After they left, a letter was received by the Board of Trustees from the farmers with a check for $25 and a note expressing their appreciation for the services and care the school had provided over the years.

The auditorium of the school was the scene for many social events through the years, like the **Colonial Ball**, attended by residents in full costume, and a dancing school for the youth of the community.

Ending a long and distinguished phase of its history, in 1991 Malaga Cove **School was closed** because of declining enrollments in the school district. In 1992 it was leased by a private school and a foreign-language school. The Rancho de los Palos Verdes Historical Society will be establishing a small museum focusing on local history in the tower building. The athletic fields will continue to be used by local sports groups.

.45 Continue on Via Almar. Turn right onto Via Arroyo after the school, and then right again into
.6 the parking lot.

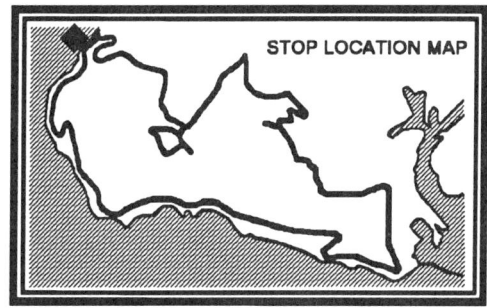

◆Stop 17.

Malaga Cove

The corner of the bluff here may be the best place to sum up the Palos Verdes experience. As you stand above sheer cliffs of Palos Verdes stone, you can observe the various forces that have combined to make the Peninsula such a **special place**. Archeological digs have shown that this spot was one of the earliest inhabited areas ever investigated in California. The buildings - the red-roofed school and the shoreside swimming pool - typify the quality of the early buildings and goals of the Palos Verdes Project. Finally, the stream of local residents trudging down the path to the beach carrying surfboards and picnics and returning with sunburns and sandy feet from the tide pools shows the appeal of the area today.

A plaque placed beside the school by the local Historical Society commemorates one of the best **archeological sites** in southern California. Excavated in 1936 by the Southwest Museum, the dig was unusual because it held four clearly separate levels indicating the presence of four successive but different groups on the site. From the items left behind, some conclusions can be drawn as to how the early residents ate, lived and organized their communities.

The lowest and oldest group of artifacts was referred to as the **Early Period**, and the people who left them behind may have been here as long as 7,000 years ago. They left small chert tools, called microliths, useful for cutting and making holes, and thousands of seashells, indicating a diet of shellfish.

The second level, called the **Millingstone Period**, had numerous stone metates, used for grinding grain and seed. There were also knife blades, shell and stone decorative items, and some mysterious disc-shaped stones that may have been used in religious ceremonies. The people were then more settled, with time to create and ornament their lives.

Above this level was a quite different assortment of artifacts: mortar and pestle grinders, bone harpoon barbs, shell fish hooks, and many bones of mammals and fish. Called the **Hunting Period**, this era (from 3,500-1,200 years ago) saw a hunting culture that combined a meat and fish diet with some sort of grain. Like the Indians further inland, they may have been dependent on the acorn, a nutritious food that requires special and complicated preparation. Whether oak trees grew on the Peninsula, however, is a subject for debate, and assumptions that the native Americans here were acorn users like the ones in the basin are not universally accepted.

Metate on display at PVIC

The **Late Prehistoric Period** (1,200 years ago until the arrival of the Europeans) was well represented at the Malaga Cove Site, with more than 15 feet of material containing artifacts, including arrowheads, bowls, mortars and pestles, fish hooks, bone tools and ornaments, and items sealed with asphaltum to make them waterproof. Some unusual small, flat, painted rocks, called gamestones, were also found, though there was no indication as to their use. Charming soapstone carvings of sea creatures showed a more advanced civilization, with time to spare for artistic pursuits.

The Native Americans did not long survive the arrival of the Spanish, and little is known of their culture. No one even knows what they called themselves, so the Indians of the basin are referred to as **Gabrieleno**, after their association with the mission at San Gabriel, and the group at Malaga Cove are called Chowigna. In the few descriptions made of them, the Gabrielenos were described as small, stocky, muscular and well-built. The women were handsome, with lovely eyes and features, and the children "fair, friendly and smiling."

Unfortunately, work on the Malaga Cove archeological site was never completed, as it was bulldozed in 1955 for a condominium project. Six years later when a neighboring home was adding a tennis court, additional artifacts were found. In 1965 a complete **skull and several bones** were found on the bluff and taken to UCLA for Carbon 14 dating, which found them to be approximately 1800 years old.

Down the cliff is the **Roessler Pool**, built in 1930 as the Palos Verdes Swim Club. The pool is 145 feet long and 45 feet wide and originally held salt water that was pumped from the ocean and warmed to 76 degrees. The five-story, pink building was designed by Kirtland Cutter, the architect who did so much of the early design work for the Project. It is being extensively renovated and will be reopened as a private club.

The first lifeguard at the pool was Grant Leehouts, a **true hero** who had saved nine men from an oil fire in San Pedro and had won surfboard races and mile-long rough-water swims. During the 30's the building held a nursery school, and during WWII it was a Hostess House for soldiers. The pool was later named for H.F.B. (Fred) Roessler, who for many years was mayor of Palos Verdes Estates. .

The trail down from the northern end of the parking lot leads to **RAT** (Right After Torrance) **Beach**, the most southerly stretch of the long beach that lines Santa Monica Bay. There is a lifeguard some distance down the beach and some interesting tide pools at the foot of the trail.

You will notice that the **beach sand** is very dark, due to the presence of heavy black minerals called ilmenite and magnetite. Currents tend to sweep the lighter quartz sand around the point, leaving the heavier dark minerals concentrated here. You will also see some exposures of the Valmonte Diatomite (a soft, white rock) near the base of the cliff. The rocks here have been tightly folded and although much of the structure is covered by landslides, you can still see almost vertical mudstone and conglomerate beds.

MILEAGE

0 **Return to the parking lot and drive down Paseo del Mar.**

House number 408, a long, low building with two royal palms flanking a rectangular lawn, was one of the **original project** houses, built in 1925 as an example of the style of house approved by the Art Jury.

.1 **Pull over to the right side of the road, in front of the Neighborhood Church.**

Today part of the **church grounds** are open to the public, including the waterfall area and a seaside balcony. On the cliff wall overlooking the ocean there is a memorial to loved ones lost at sea. On Sundays, Docent-led tours are available; call for more information (978-9353).

The Neighborhood Church occupies a grand mansion built in 1928 for **J.J. Haggerty**, the owner of Haggerty's exclusive New York and Los Angeles department stores. Haggerty wanted nothing but the best. He imported artisans and painters from Italy to create ceiling murals, carved balustrades, a huge baronial fireplace, wrought-iron gates, and monogrammed decorations everywhere. The house stretched for 290 feet and had 20 rooms, 2 garages, a large double conservatory, subterranean lodge, trophy room, and a drawing room 28 by 63 feet.

The **grounds** were equally spectacular. There was a 30-foot-thick sea wall, an outdoor swimming pool, a miniature golf course, and gardens designed by Olmstead which had waterfalls, lily ponds and walkways. A pier extended into the ocean, falsely rumored to be used for smuggling.

Unfortunately, Mrs. Haggerty never liked the place and the family spent most of their time at their homes in Los Angeles and Long Beach. It was eventually sold to financier Harry Wheeler who decorated it in his own unique style, consisting largely of representations of the unclothed female figure. To

MILEAGE Wheeler, **no nudes were bad nudes**. He had statues in the gardens and stairwells, bronze and silver lamp bases, and paintings of nude women everywhere. For some reason Mrs. Wheeler too preferred their other home.

After Wheeler's death in the late 40's, the house was put on the market for $250,000. By 1950 it had

Ceiling detail from the Church

been reduced by half but still no buyers were interested. Finally the members of the **Neighborhood Church** made an offer of $60,000 which was accepted. An auction was held to dispose of the works of art, which included bedroom sets from the palaces of Louis 14th, 15th and 16th; art objects from the palace of Czar Nicholas; 18th century English silver, and a hand-tufted Austrian rug 57 feet long valued at $40,000. The Palos Verdes Homes Association placed many conditions on the approval, but finally in 1952 the beautiful seaside mansion became the home of the Neighborhood Church.

On the opposite side of the street, house number 424, a two-story white building, was also one of the early **sample houses** put up by the Palos Verdes Project, this one in 1927.

.7 **Continue on Paseo del Mar up the hill. You will pass 3 houses on the right side of the road, and then you will see an open space with large rocks, and a chain blocking vehicle access to the trail down to the beach. Park on the side of the road.**

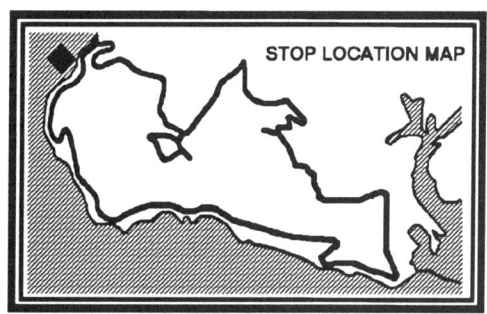

◆Stop 18.
Bluff Cove

From this **vantage point** you can see all of the coast north of Los Angeles, from Malibu to Point Dume. On a clear day the Santa Monica Mountains appear to be right next door.

The road down to the shore is steep but even, though channels are often washed into the surface. The cliff faces are very steep so be careful not to go too close to the edge.

This cove has always been a popular spot with **surfers**, for the waves roll in tall and steady. In the early days of the Project, the cove was nicknamed Little Waikiki and was a favorite spot for Grant Leehouts, lifeguard at the pool, to bring the local boys to try out their hand-carved redwood surfboards. During the 40's a local surfing group, called the Malahinis, built a shelter at the beach, gave dances there, and surfed in the moonlight. Today the local surfers are known for their territoriality and their purist attitude to the sport.

Somewhere off the coast here lies a mysterious group of stones known as the **Chinese anchors**. Divers from

"Chinese Anchor" at PVIC

Redondo Beach found the pile of about 50 rounded stones several years ago. Each one has a smooth hole through the center, weighs from 280 to 1,000 pounds, and is pocked with holes from ocean creatures and weathering.

Numerous **theories** have been proposed to explain the stones. One is that they are from a Chinese junk that sank off the Peninsula some 3,500 years ago. In support of this theory, some scientists claim to have matched the mineral content of the stones with a formation in China. Other scientists say that the rock is very like the local Monterrey formation and that the stones were anchors used by 19th century local fishermen of Chinese descent. Yet another theory says that the stones were made and used by Portuguese whalers during the last century to anchor whale carcasses offshore. Whatever the explanation, even the exact location of the stones remains a mystery to all but their discoverers. One of the stones is on display at the Interpretive Center if you want to come up with your own explanation.

Across the cove you can see a very steep cliff face, traversed by Palos Verdes Drive West. Creating this road was one of the early triumphs of the Project. **Road building** was difficult: mule teams pulling scoops called Fresnos began the job, followed by wagons to haul away the dirt. Finally, asphalt was laid over a rock base. As with every aspect of the Project, the planners considered aesthetic qualities when designing the road system, choosing curved roads and decorative wooden signs, and forbidding billboards.

The section of the road you can see was the most difficult challenge. The cliff there was the tallest on the Peninsula, over 420 feet high, and the road was too steep to be practical. At the top stood a concrete marker, labelled "Douglas", used for surveying purposes. In 1923 workers blasted out the cliff face, creating what was called the **Douglas Cut**. More than 20,000 people came to watch the explosion, which used 60 tons of blasting powder. Afterwards the Project salesmen undoubtedly tried to sell the spectators building lots.

This small section of road cost $90,000 for the removal of 300,000 cubic yards of dirt, but it cut almost two miles off the

route and reduced it to a level grade. Some of the rock fell to the cove where it created a new shoreline, while the rest was removed for use in further road building. In 1925 both Western and Hawthorne Avenues were extended to the Peninsula, and one year later the entire **circular route** was finished. To celebrate, 300 automobiles from towns all over the South Bay drove in a procession from Redondo Beach to San Pedro, a distance of just under 20 miles.

MILEAGE

**Continue up the hill and around the curve on 0
Paseo del Mar. This road was washed out (and
several houses destroyed) by shore slumping so**

MILEAGE **you must take a slight detour.**

.1 **When you face the "Not a Through Street" sign, take a hard left. This takes you back to Palos Verdes Drive West, where you turn right.**

The homes on your right belong to the City of Palos Verdes Estates which purchased them as part of the settlement of a lawsuit centering around whether it had maintained a storm drain adequately. Now city officials enjoy a splendid view of the ocean as an employee benefit.

.4 **Continue for .3 mile and then bear right on Paseo del Mar.**

.8 **Along the right side of the road you will pass the Palos Verdes Shoreline Preserve.** There is parking and a trail along the cliff top. Pull over and stop on the right side of the road.

Just below is the area chosen by Francis B. "Dry-Dock" Smith, a noted harbor engineer, as the best site for a **yacht harbor**. He was retained by the Pacific Coast Yacht Club, formed in 1927 by a group of wealthy yacht enthusiasts. A sketch of the build-

.8 ing they planned shows an enormous, grandiose, cliff-hugging structure topped with a multi-storied tower. Access to the boathouses, promenade and docks was to be provided by elevators. A breakwater long enough to enclose 66 acres of water was part of the plan, with protected mooring spaces for 400 boats. The club did hold a regatta in 1927, with a two-day race to Catalina, but their other plans never came to pass.

Many of the great plans of the Palos Verdes Project were abandoned because of **the Depression.** Since many of the residents were relatively wealthy, it took some time for the country's financial reverses to have an effect, but by 1932 the Homes Association was unable to pay county taxes on its properties.

Attempts were made to cut costs, but by 1933 changes in tax policy had further reduced income to the Homes Association.

From 1932 to 1937 no new residents built homes on the Peninsula, but life went on for the original group. The **Palos Verdes Women's Club** provided oranges for breakfast and hot lunches (using vegetables donated by the Japanese farmers) for children of the unemployed in Harbor City and set up a food depot in Redondo Beach.

By 1938 things looked bad for the Project, now called Palos Verdes Estates, Inc. The Homes Association owed more than $62,000 (including almost $34,000 in **back taxes** to LA County) and had few resources. The County Auditor proposed that the Homes Association turn over the title to their parklands in return for cancellation of the taxes. A public auction of the parks, Country Club and other community properties was threatened for February of 1939. After much discussion, the County offered a slightly better deal: cancellation of taxes in return for Bluff Cove and the beaches west of it, through the Douglas Cut to Lunada Bay (all of the area included in this chapter of the driving tour, some deal!), to be used as Country parkland.

Most residents were strongly opposed, particularly to surrendering Bluff Cove, although others felt that the title didn't matter as long as it remained parkland. A committee of residents was empowered to represent the citizens in what was called the "**Parklands Controversy**", and after much deliberation determined to offer only Lunada Bay to the County. However, when they met again with County authorities, the County had lost interest in the entire deal.

One suggestion made by the citizens committee was that Palos Verdes Estates become an incorporated **city of the sixth class**, which would eliminate taxes on the parklands. Strong opposition to incorporation

MILEAGE

.8

MILEAGE was expressed by newspapers, banks and other civic groups who felt that becoming a city would mean giving up their traditional, personal control.

In July of 1939 an **auction** disposed of all the unsold lots held by Palos Verdes, Inc. One lot on Paseo del Mar sold for $40 plus $281 in back taxes. A 157-acre parcel in Upper Lunada Bay sold for $4,000 plus almost $10,000 in taxes. This sale did, however, provide enough new landowners in favor of incorporation to complete the necessary petition, and an election was ordered.

The young community was torn apart by the controversy and much bitterness was felt. Finally, on December 9, 1939, in a vote of 213-206, incorporation was passed and **Palos Verdes Estates became an official city.** Miraleste, on the other side of the Peninsula, was not included. The financial problems of the city were not solved immediately, but the parklands were saved and over time the city has succeeded in combining fiscal prudence with preservation of the Project's original goals.

.9 Behind you the large house with the copper roof (the second one from the overlook) was the subject of national media attention when its construction was incomplete after nearly a decade of work by its owners. City regulations require that houses be completed in a certain amount of time, and after years of complaints by residents tired of looking at scaffolding, the City threatened to have the **house razed** if it wasn't finished. The owners quickly brought it close enough to a finished state to satisfy the city and the magazine reporters departed.

3.0 Continue for 2.2 miles along Paseo del Mar, past Rocky Point Road and Yarmouth Road. On your right you will see a grassy area, with large boulders lining the road. Park on the roadside. If you plan to take the trail down to the cove, continue
3.5 to the far end of the grassy area.

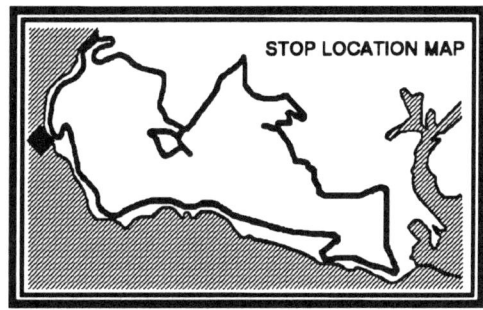

◆Stop 19.

Lunada Bay

From this **vantage point** you can look down into Lunada Bay, a nearly perfect semicircle between two points - Rocky Point (also called Palos Verdes Point) to the right and Resort Point to the left.

During World War II, concern about the possibility of an attack from the ocean intensified. **Gun emplacements** were set up on the coast so as to leave no stretch unprotected. On Rocky Point the army constructed one of its heavy batteries. Three giant 155 mm guns were placed on concrete mounts, underground ammunition storage rooms were built, and tunnels were constructed connecting the various rooms. Above you, at the end of Punta Place, a permanent artillery observation station was also built.

In 1942 the army decided that the coastline of Palos Verdes Estates had to be guarded night and day. Surfers and swimmers were told that they could no longer use the beaches. **Photographing** the coastline was **prohibited.** No longer could camera-toting surfers ride into the Peninsula's most sensitive coves.

Almost 20 years later, on March 16, 1961, one of the most dramatic events on the Peninsula took place, when the freighter **Dominator ran aground** on Rocky Point. The ship was carrying 9000 pounds of grain from Vancouver, British

Columbia, to Algiers, and was hugging the coast due to fog.

For a week after the crash attempts were made to drag the ship free, but all failed. Hundreds of thousands of **sightseers** came from all over Los Angeles, causing immense traffic jams and serious property damage in the area. The City Council finally approved a plan to remove the grain onto barges, and the salvaging process was begun but it met with only limited success.

In November the freighter broke in two. By May of the following year the rotting grain was supporting an enormous breeding colony of **flies**, and the County Health Department came and sprayed it, and then covered it with tarp and insecticide. Through the years two men died exploring the wreck and eight sightseeing boats were lost near it.

In 1974 after more than a hundred wrecked cars were removed from the P.V. beaches by giant Sikorsky helicopters, the possibility of removing the last of the Dominator was examined and dismissed. A big storm in 1981 washed 43

more cars offshore and removed some of the Dominator **wreckage**. Today the last portion of the Dominator remains on the point, visible during low tide.

Looking out at the ocean you can see the beds of giant **kelp**, a greenish-brown seaweed, growing offshore. This plant is the fastest growing known, increasing in length by as much as 20 inches in one day. Small feet, called holdfasts, attach the plants to the rocks; the stems and blades grow upward, supported by gas-filled floats at the base of the blades.

Kelp beds are harvested by special ships something like lawnmowers that cut the tops off the plants and send the kelp into holds on conveyor belts. The kelp is processed to produce **algin**, an ingredient in ice cream, beer, adhesives, textile dying, and many more food and consumer products. The plant is able to regenerate quickly since only its top few feet are removed.

The kelp beds were in serious danger, however, during the 1970's, due to pollution and attack from **sea urchins** (who eat the stem above the holdfast). In an interesting example of the balance of nature, the urchins were proliferating in part because their main predators, sea otters, were disappearing due to hunting and habitat changes. Once the pollution of the water was decreased and the sea urchins controlled, the kelp beds began to return. This was good news for fish and fishermen, since the beds are home to mackerel, bonita, barracuda, yellowtail, white sea bass, halibut, opal eye and turbot. Thresher shark (used mostly by McDonald's) also live around the kelp.

Another, perhaps more significant reason for the decline of the kelp beds was **offshore pollution**. The Palos Verdes Peninsula has the dubious distinction of having the world's largest deposit of DDT in an arc around its perimeter. This was deposited by the world's largest producer of DDT, which was located in Carson. Some of the material ended up in the sewer system, was transported into the ocean off of White Point via a pipe (called the White Point outfall, still in use), and was spread by currents around the Peninsula. The chemical plant was closed down in the fifties, and gradually the DDT became covered with sediments.

Government agencies are now feuding over whether it is desirable to leave some solid material in the treated waste water sent back to the ocean via the outfall to keep the DDT covered. All involved are also suing each other over the costs of cleaning up the DDT still in the pipes and on the site of the former factory. Some have suggested that the DDT be removed, but this would reintroduce it into the ecosystem and would create many tons of hazardous waste to be carried away. The DDT does deteriorate, however, and in about 150 years should have virtually disappeared.

At the south end of the grassy area there is a steep and very difficult **pathway** down to the shore. There you will find some fascinating tide pools in the exposures of dark igneous basalts and lighter beds of mudstone.

There are three sections of the **tide pools**, cleverly called high-tide, mid-tide and low-tide zones, each one supporting a different population of creatures. The best time, of course, to explore tide pools is at low tide when they are fully exposed.

If you are not planning to visit the tide pools and are not interested in reading about the creatures you might find there, **jump** to the end of this chapter.

One of the first creatures you will see is the snail, with its spiral shell. **Snails** travel by pushing their muscular feet forward, in search of algae and seaweed to eat. When disturbed, the snail pulls its entire body into the shell and closes the opening with its operculum, a horny trap-door-like plate. The most common types here are turban snails (dark black, brown or purple with a shiny apex), periwinkles (brown with faint white markings) and the scaled tube worm shell (a twisty white tube).

Some snail shells may fool you, for they have become home to the **hermit crab**, which is actually more like a shrimp than a crab. This creature inserts its back half into a borrowed shell for protection and scurries through the tide pools searching for food.

Sea stars, aenemones, urchins and mussels all share the tidepools.

Other crabs include the lined shore crab (reddish purple with black-green lines, up to 2" long), purple shore crab (purple with darker spots), and the lumpy crab (red brown with bumps). Their thin bodies can slide between rocks where they hide, waiting for plankton and other food.

Barnacles are the short white towers that cluster on rocks, ships, animals and shells all over the shore. When a wave washes over them they reach out their feathery feet to catch plankton washing by. Acorn barnacles (white) are the most common, though you will also see brown buckshot barnacles (brown and small, with a cross in the closed top). In the mussel beds you will see gooseneck barnacles which look more like shells, with many white plates on top of a grayish green neck.

Limpets have flattish, one-piece shells less than an inch across that are fastened tight to the rock. They scrape algae off the rocks as they move very slowly about. At night they return to the same resting spot, which through many years may become a deep indentation. Their relative, the abalone, is much larger (up to 8"), and hides in deep crevices and under ledges. Abalone are protected by law now, since they are endangered by hungry divers, competition for food with sea urchins, and pollution. The inside of their shells (which are often found around this cove) is a lovely iridescent pearly color.

Although you may not see a related creature called the **piddock clam**, its presence is evident from the holes that pit the rocks along the shore. This clam attaches itself to rocks with a suckerlike foot, and then uses its serrated shell to burrow into the rock. It lives its life inside the rock, feeding by means of siphons. Occasionally a clam will drill completely through a rock, leaving a tidy tube from one side of the rock to another.

One of the most successful of ocean creatures is the sea urchin, with its thin purple (or red) shell covered with spines. **Urchins** travel on long flexible suction feet and also make indentations in rocks. They are very efficient feeders, competing with neighbors like the abalone. They pull their bodies against their prey with tube feet, then gnaw the food with a toothed organ called Aristotle's Lantern in the center of their basal opening. They sometimes eat the stem of the kelp plant, thus cutting it loose and killing it. In some cultures urchins are a taste treat, and are harvested as a main course.

The prettiest tide-pool dweller is the **anemone**, which looks like a multi-petalled flower. It pulls water into its body, stinging and paralyzing creatures that come along with it. Their sting is generally harmless to humans but can cause an allergic reaction in some people. When touched, the anemone will close up into a grayish-green lump stuck with bits of shell.

The anemone can move very slowly along the rocks, sliding on its base, or release itself to swim through the water.

Other creatures you might see in these tide pools include chitons (slug-like molluscs with eight scaly plates down their backs), sea slugs (multicolored slugs up to 3" long), sea stars (often called starfish, brightly colored and fancy in design), and isopods (14-legged crustaceans with plated bodies).

Without **plants** in the tide pools all these animals would have no source of food. The most common part of the ocean's vegetable soup are the algaes, like sponge weed (green, with branched arms), sea lettuce (green with wide flat leaves), moss weed (green and feathery), kelp, rock weed (greenish brown, with little floats on the branches), and coralline algae (pink-lavender stacks of little cups or flat plates on rocks). The only common non-algae is sea grass, like bright green wet crabgrass.

The **ecosystem** of the tide pools is fragile; each creature depends on having clean water, a steady food supply, and a home safe from predators. Be careful, therefore, not to interfere with their lives. Do not remove living creatures and do not throw trash or food into the pools. Leave empty shells in the pools so that they can become homes for hermit crabs. Also be careful when out on the points; high tide can come upon you suddenly and rare rogue waves have swept people offshore. When scrambling on the rocks remember that the green rocks are the slipperiest.

MILEAGE

At the northern end of the overlook area, turn left onto Avenida Mirola. Go two blocks (.3 mile) .   0

Turn left onto Via Anacapa.   .3

Follow Via Anacapa .3 mile until you reach the side of Lunada Bay Plaza. Turn right on Yarmouth Road and immediately right again onto Palos Verdes Drive West.   .6

Turn right into the parking lot in front of the Lunada Bay Patio Building.   .7

◆Stop 20.

Lunada Bay Plaza

The original plan for this plaza called for "**a bit of old Spain** set down on the sheltered coast of Palos Verdes," but the Depression eliminated this project along with so many others. The planners called for a number of two-story buildings with tall towers, linked by an arcade like that at Malaga Cove.

Tile detail in the Plaza

It was not until 1966 that this Mediterranean-style **plaza** was constructed, and although it is very true in style to the original plans, it is much smaller in scale. The plaza today has a charming 5000-square-foot interior courtyard with an ornate fountain. Restaurants and shops line the courtyard, while offices occupy the second story. Other businesses are located around the plaza on neighboring streets.

The fountain in the small park that faces the plaza was installed in 1963 by the Palos Verdes Garden Club. Called la **Fuente de los Niños**, or the Children's Fountain, it was funded by donations from more than 250 local chil- dren, whose names are sealed into the stone of its base. The fountain is dedicated to the memory of Brooks Snelgrove, Build- ing Commis- sioner of the Pa- los Verdes Project and twice Presi- dent of the Homes As- sociation.

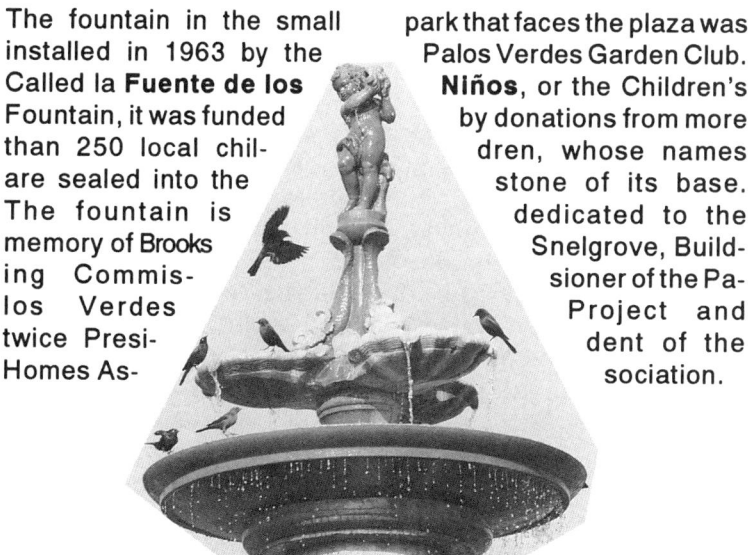

	MILEAGE
Turn right onto Palos Verdes Drive West and continue back to the Point Vicente Interpretive Center.	**0**
After .5 mile you will cross **Paseo Lunado**. Its green median strip covers a large drainage tunnel. At times sea lions come into Lunada Bay and their roaring, amplified by the tunnel, is heard throughout the neighborhood.	**.5**

As you drive along, you may notice that the hillsides are stepped, or terraced. These **terraces** are the result of successive periods of land uplift, as sea level changed and the land rose. The Peninsula has always been higher than the surrounding area, its hard basement rock keeping it from eroding to a flatland. Just by existing, it has protected the Los Angeles shoreline and kept the beaches in exist- ence. At one time the Peninsula was an island, much like Catalina today, separated from the mainland by a wide channel of water.

As changes in the crust of the earth caused the land

MILEEAGE	here to rise, the Peninsula slowly emerged from the ocean. The speed at which the land rose varied over the millenia, and although it never stopped completely, during the years when the **uplift** was slow the ocean cut level beaches backed by cliffs around the land mass. Thirteen major terraces have been formally identified, though many more transitional stages can be described. The upper terraces have been modified by the effects of time - erosion, landslides and house building - and it is the lower ones that are best preserved. You are driving on terrace four; Crest Road is on terrace ten; terrace thirteen is the highest, at San Pedro Hill.
	The mild, nearly perfect **weather** in Palos Verdes is a result of the unique temperature inversions caused by the geographic peculiarities of the area. High pressures along the coast cause air to sink slowly down from above, warming as it sinks. This is called an inversion layer and is what traps pollution in the basin and creates the Santa Ana hot dry winds. In Palos Verdes the cool air produced by ocean currents slides up under the warm layer, bringing fog and pleasant evening temperatures.
	Very often **temperatures** will rise steadily as one ascends the hill. Sometimes a layer of clouds will mark the boundary between the two air layers, so that one can drive from fog into sunshine by driving up or down the hill. Although it varies considerably from place to place on the Peninsula, in general residents regard the weather as virtually perfect; few months have even three days when the sun does not appear.
.9	You will cross from Palos Verdes Estates into Rancho Palos Verdes.
1.6	On the hill to your left is the Los Verdes **Golf Course.** You can see the giant net erected to prevent golf balls from arriving uninvited into neighboring homes.

The park above the golf course, Hesse Park, was the **Palos Verdes blue butterfly**, a small (1"+) bright silvery blue creature. It had been found in ten locations on the Peninsula, but by 1978 it had been declared an endangered species and by 1980 the areas where it did its fluttering had been declared critical habitats, requiring special management.

MILEEAGE
1.7

Being a fussy type, this very particular butterfly would eat only the seeds of one plant, the astragalas (also called locoweed or rattleweed). When what appeared to be weeds were mistakenly cleared from the grounds of the park, the butterfly's **habitat** was **destroyed** there. Unfortunately, the butterfly seemed to die out in other locations as well. In 1986 Rancho Palos Verdes had the dubious distinction of being the first city sued by the Federal government for destroying a critical habitat, though the suit was later thrown out of court. Local lepidopterists hope that the Palos Verdes Blue Butterfly is just laying low and will reappear now that astragalas has been replanted.

After Palos Verdes Estates became incorporated in 1939 the rest of the Peninsula had to develop independently. For many years the areas of Rolling Hills and Miraleste had their own identity but no legal standing, while much of the rest of the Peninsula still belonged to Frank Vanderlip and the Palos Verdes Corporation. In 1953 all the remaining land on the Peninsula (except land kept by the Vanderlips in the Portuguese Bend area), some 7000 acres, was sold to the **Great Lakes Carbon Corporation**, which had been mining the diatomaceous earth on the northern edge of the Peninsula. Though they had originally planned to do further mining near the crest, they instead began developing their land, introducing tract housing and changing the Peninsula forever.

In 1957 both Rolling Hills and Rolling Hills Estates incorporated to provide **local control** for the residents. Much of the coastal area, however, was left unprotected from development. A local group, called

MILEEAGE "Save Our Coastline," was formed, and in 1972 voters throughout the state established the Coastal Commission, which regulated and controlled development along the entire state's 1,100 mile oceanfront. The jurisdiction of the commission included new housing, businesses and other development in a strip that varied in width from 1,000 yards to five miles from the shoreline.

1.8 Continue through the intersection at the bottom of Hawthorne Boulevard. The Golden Cove Center is on your left.

Although the Coastal Commission was a positive response to voters' concerns about **development**, its restrictions were not strict enough to suit many on the Peninsula. Grading across from the Golden Cove Center (still visible) shows the extent of development approved by the County and permitted by the Coastal Commission. Drilling for oil was also going on at the same time at Long Point and Point Fermin and although only traces of oil and asphalt were found the possibility of oil wells made residents nervous.

Realizing that it was the only way to maintain local control of development, residents on the remaining Peninsula land finally joined together and incorporated in 1973, choosing as their name a shortened version of the original Sepulveda land grant, Rancho de los Palos Verdes, and becoming the **City of Rancho Palos Verdes**. One of the first actions of the new city was to stop development across from Golden Cove, and in the Paseo del Mar area east of the landslide.

The new city rezoned all the vacant lands along the coast at a density of one residential unit per buildable acre. For many years it was not economical to develop at that density, but in recent years rising house prices have stimulated new proposals for the

1.9 coastal areas. The area on your right received

approval in 1991 for 86 homes, with more than 60
acres left as parkland, habitat for the gnatcatcher (a
small bird that may be offically listed as an endangered species within the next few years), wetland preserve and open space. Trails will extend the length of the bluff and there will be public parking. The Coastal Commission approved this project.

Today Rancho Palos Verdes, with a population of around 41,000, is the largest of the **five communities** on the Peninsula. Palos Verdes Estates, with a population of almost 15,000 is next, followed by Rolling Hills Estates (population just over 8,000) and Rolling Hills (population almost 2,000). Two areas, Academy Hill and Westfield, remain unincorporated. San Pedro, the fifth community, is actually a part of the City of Los Angeles though it retains its own local sense of identity and history.

Turn right into the Point Vicente Interpretive Center. 2.3

The Palos Verdes Peninsula will remain "A Place Set Apart." With its sunshine and seacliffs, its dreamers and developers, its fountains and farms, it will always be something special to those lucky enough to live, work and visit here.

Handicapped Access

Stop 1. Point Vicente Interpretive Center - The museum building (except the tower) is accessible, including the restrooms, which have their entrances outside the building. Several of the paths through the grounds, including the one to the terrace in back, are level and paved.

Stop 2. Fishing Access Parking Lot - Both the lot and the restrooms are accessible.

Stop 3. Wayfarers Chapel - The Chapel and Visitor Center (including the restrooms) are all accessible.

Stop 4. Forrestal Drive - Some of the exposed geology could be seen from the paved road. The Ladera Linda Community Center and the Discovery Room are accessible.

Stop X. Short Cut - This is just a driving stop.

Stop 5. White Point - The pathway to the top of the cliff would not be accessible but quite a lot can be seen from the parking area. There are paved roads extending all along the cove if you take the road down to the state park.

Stop 6. Point Fermin - All the pathways in the park are level and paved.

Stop 7. Angels Gate - There is access to the Korean Bell and the Information Center. Access to the gun emplacements and the military museum would be possible when the second drive is open, Saturdays and Sundays from 12:00-5:00.

Stop 8. Gaffey Overlook - The overlook parking lot is level.

Stop 9. Georgeff Canyon - Much of the view can be seen from the car.

Stop 10. General Store - The store and surrounding area are all level.

Stop 11. Botanic Garden - Everything is accessible.

Stop 12. Del Cerro - This would be difficult. To see the view requires climbing a small hill. There are no paved paths though the ground is fairly smooth.

Stop 13. Indian Peak - Most of the view can be seen from the car.

Stop 14. Silver Spur - Most of the view can be seen from the car.

Stop 15. La Venta - Most of the view can be seen from the car.

Stop 16. Malaga Cove Plaza - The plaza is level and easily accessible.

Stop 17. Malaga Cove - Most of the points of interest can been seen from the parking lot.

Stop 18. Bluff Cove - Some of the cove can be seen from the car. The view is better if you go 10-15 feet on a dirt surface, to a point where you can see down into the cove.

Stop 19. Lunada Bay - You can see some of the cove from the car. A better view is available if you go 20-30 feet over a grassy surface to the top of the cliff.

Stop 20. Lunada Bay Plaza - You can see almost everything discussed on this stop from the car. The courtyard of the Patio Building is accessible via an elevator from the rear parking lot. Most of the other businesses in the area are at street level.

Bibliography
of The Palos Verdes Peninsula
With Thanks to Carmen Marinella

Almeida, Arthur; Almeida, Irene; et al. The Vincent Thomas Bridge, San Pedro's Golden Gate. San Pedro Historical Society.

Bauer, Helen. California Indian Days. Garden City, NY: Doubleday, 1963.

Bauman, Gus. History of Palos Verdes Estates, California. Palos Verdes Estates, CA: 1975.

Dana, Richard Henry. Two Years Before the Mast. New York: Washington Square Press, Inc., 1968. First published:1840.

Fink, Augusta. Time and the Terraced Land. Berkeley, CA.: Howell North Books, 1966.

Fink, Augusta. Palos Verdes Peninsula: Time and the Terraced Land. Santa Cruz, CA: Western Tanager Press, 1987.

Flaherty, Joseph. An End and a Beginning. The South Coast and Los Angeles, 1850-1887. Jerico, NY; Exposition Press, 1972.

Frick, John. Wildflowers of Catalina. Avalon, CA: Portmanteau, 1975.

Gales, Donald Moore. Handbook of Wildflowers, Weeds, Wildlife, and Weather of the Palos Verdes Peninsula. Palos Verdes Peninsula, CA: FoldaRoll Company, 1988.

Gillingham, Robert Cameron. The Rancho San Pedro; the Story of a Famous Rancho in Los Angeles County and Its

Owners the Dominguez Family. rev.ed. California Museum Reproductions, 1983.

Grenier, Judson A., with Robert C. Gillingham. California Legacy, The James Alexander Watson-Maria Dolores Dominguez de Watson Family. Watson Land Company, CA: 1987.

Hansen, A.E. Rolling Hills: The Early Years, February 1930 Through December 4, 1941. Rolling Hills, CA: 1978.

Heizer, Robert F. and Elasser, Albert B. The Natural World of the California Indians. Berkeley, Los Angeles: University of California Press, 1980.

Hinton, Sam. Seashore Life of Southern California. University of California Press, 1969.

Jepson, Willis Linn. A Manual of the Flowering Plants of Califonia. Berkeley and Los Angeles: University of California Press, 1960.

Johnson, Ken. Fun, Frustration and Fulfillment; an Historical Study of the City of Redondo Beach. Redondo Beach, CA: 1965.

Johnston, Bernice Eastman. California's Gabrieleno Indians. Los Angeles: The Southwest Museum, 1962.

Krythe, Maymie. Port Admiral Phineas Banning 1830-1885. California Historical Society. Los Angeles. CA: Anderson, Ritchie & Simmin, 1957.

Morgan, Delane. The Palos Verdes Story. Palos Verdes Estates, CA: The Palos Verdes Review, 1982.

Murphy, Don. The Ranchos: Peninsula Sketches. Don Murphy Enterprises, 1987.

Queenan, Charles F. The Port of Los Angeles from Wilderness to World Port. Los Angeles, CA: Los Angeles Harbor Department, 1983.

Reiter, Martin. The Palos Verdes Peninsula; a Geologic Guide and More. Dubuque, Iowa: Kendall Hunt Publishing Co.: 1984.

Silka, Henry P. San Pedro; A Pictorial History. San Pedro, CA: San Pedro Historical Society, 1984.

Smith, Sarah Bixby. Adobe Days. Fresno, CA: Valley Publishers, 1974.

Snyderman, Marty. California Marine Life. Marcor Publishing, 1988.

Swaffield, Roland G. Saga of the City of Rolling Hills (Old Rolling Hills). Long Beach, CA: Crawford Press, 1958.

Thacker, Mary Eva. "History of Los Palos Verdes Rancho, 1542-1923." M.A. Thesis: The Graduate School of the University of Southern California, Los Angeles, CA: 1923.

Trejos, Charlotte M. My Carson, Your Carson, A Picture Book of Past and Present. Carson, CA: Trejos Literary Agency, 1987.

Vanderlip, Frank A. and Boyden Sparks. From Farm Boy to Financier. New York: C. Appleton-Century, 1935.

Vickery, Oliver. Harbor Heritage. Mountain View, CA: Morgan Press Farag Associates, 1979.

Young, Donald. Wartime Palos Verdes. Torrance, CA, 1985.

Other Sources

Our Town. Rolling Hills Estates, CA: Supplement to the Palos Verdes Peninsula News, 1987-1992.

Palos Verdes Review. Palos Verdes Estates, CA: Review Publications, 1986-1992.

Peninsula Panorama. Torrance, CA: Supplement to the Copley Los Angeles Newspapers: The Daily Breeze. 1987-1992.

INDEX

Abalone 51
Abalone Cove 24, 54
Abalone Cove Shoreline Park 20
Agua Negra Canyon 86
Altamira Shale 25, 49
American Cetacean Society 10, 47, 48
Angels Gate Cultural Center 59
Angels Gate Park 59
Animal care center 19
Animals: coys 69; gophers 49; opossums 70; raccoons 69; skunks 70
Aqua Negra Canyon 94
Archeological sites 20, 119, 119–121, 121
Art Jury 103, 112, 113
Baldwin, Lucky 89
Banning family 15
Banning Phineas T.: early history 49, 61; death 63; accomplishments 62, 71
Benedict, Harry 25, 91
Birds 10; cormorants 9; pelicans 9; seagulls 10
Bixby, George H. 68, 88
Bixby, Jotham 53, 83
Bixby Ranch 51
Blimps 100
Bluff Cove 129
Buckwheat 38
Bunkers 55
Butterflies 38, 53, 141
Cabrillo Fault 70
Cabrillo, Juan Rodriguez 15, 49, 54
Cabrillo Marine Museum 60
Cactus 38
Casa del Portal 113
Castor bean 39

Catalina Island 14, 15, 61
Catalina Schist 25, 69
Chadwick School 85
Cheney, Charles (Harry) 84, 102, 109, 110, 114
Children 7, 30
Childrens' Fountain 139
Chinese anchors 125
Clay 25, 31
Coastal areas 35, 141, 142
Coastal bluff habitat 35
Coastal Commission 19, 35, 142, 143
Coastal defense 13, 54, 55, 131
Coastal sage scrub habitat 32, 86
Commonwealth 101–102
Conservancy: Palos Verdes Peninsula Land 28, 35; Santa Catalina 15
Cox, Narcissa Vanderlip 22
Crenshaw Boulevard 26
Crystals 16, 30, 32
DDT 9, 10, 133, 134
Deep Valley 94
Del Cerro Park 87
Depression 22, 54, 65, 67, 91, 107, 108, 128
Development 20, 30, 35, 51, 64, 84, 96, 142
Diatomaceous earth 72, 82
Dominator 131-133
Dominguez, Cristobal 50
Dominguez family 49, 50, 52
Dominguez, Juan Jose 49, 50
Douglas Cut 126
Earthquakes 70
Elephant seal 17
Endangered species 9, 17, 143

Eucalyptus trees 83, 86, 104, 116
Extinction 17
Farmery 83
Farnham Martin Park 110
Father Junipero Serra 49
Fennel 91
Fire 34, 96, 97
Fishing Access Parking Lot 14
Flowers 20, 53
Flying Triangle 85, 87
Forrestal Drive 30
Fort MacArthu 57
Fort MacArthur 13, 19, 54, 57, 66
Fort MacArthur Military Museum 56
Fossils 32
Fuente de los Niños 139
Gabions 26, 28
Gaffey, John T. 66
Gaffey Street Overlook 60
Gardner Building 112, 113
Geology 25, 31, 32, 36, 49, 69, 140
Ghosts 12
Golf courses 19, 28, 54, 84, 105, 140
Gophers 49
Grandview Park 105
Grasses 39
Great Lakes Carbon Company 72, 82, 141
Grunions 50
Gun emplacements 13, 55, 131
Gutierrez, Manuel 49, 50, 52
Hansen, A.E. 83
Harden, Edward 25, 91
Harry Benedict 91
Hatano, James 54
Hesse Park 140
Historic buildings 105, 106, 107, 108, 109

Ishibash, Mas 53
Ishibashi, Annie 20, 53
Ishibashi, James 20, 53
Japanese, evacuation 52,118; farming 20, 51, 52, 53; fishing 51; history 51–53, 118, 129
Jester, Ralph 22
José, Juan Dominguez 49
Kelp 28, 133
Klondike Canyon 30
Knezevich, John J. 85
Korean Friendship Bell 54-56, 58, 59
Korean War Memorial 59
L.A. air raid 100
L.A. Harbor: future plans 65; history 62-65
La Venta Inn 106, 108, 112
Ladera Linda Community Center 30
Landfills 83-85
Landslide abatement 26
Landslides 23, 24, 26; Abalone Cove 24, 87; ancient 24, 36; PointFermin 48; Portuguese Bend 25, 87; South Shores 36
Lawsuits 26
Lewis, E.G. 101
Lighthouses: ghosts 12; Point Fermin 49, 53; Point Vicente 12
Limpets 136
Livingston Quarries 31
Local History Room 111
Long Beach earthquake 52, 116
Long Point 15, 19, 142
Los Angeles-San Pedro Railroad 62
Lunada Bay 131
Lunada Bay Plaza 138
Malaga Canyon 104, 115

Malaga Cove 104, 121
Malaga Cove Plaza 114
Malaga Cove School 116, 118
Malage Cove Library 110
Marine Mammal Care
  Center 19, 59
Marineland 14, 18, 19, 20
Martin, Farnham B. 110
Martingale Park 68
Marymount College 37, 40
Medawar, Michel 98
Military defenses 13, 54,
  54, 105, 131
Miraleste 67, 102, 141
Moss, Agnes 97
Movies 19, 23, 47, 91, 107
Museums 7, 56, 93, 118
Mustard 92
Native Americans 7, 14,
  20, 71, 120, 121
Native plants 8,
  9, 15, 27, 32, 35, 37-39, 92
Nature preserve 28
Neighborhood
  Church 122, 122–124, 124
Neptune Fountain 114
Nike missiles 13, 57
Norris Theater 97
Olmstead Brothers 88,
  91, 102, 104, 116, 123
Opossums 70
Palos Verdes Art Center 86
Palos Verdes College 86
Palos Verdes Country
  Club 105
Palos Verdes Es-
  tates 52, 67, 84,
  85, 102, 103, 128, 129,
  130, 141, 143
Palos Verdes Fault 70
Palos Verdes Library District 111
Palos Verdes Memorial Garden 115

Palos Verdes Peninsula 7,
  25, 51, 133, 143
Palos Verdes Peninsula High
  School 98–99
Palos Verdes News 85
Palos Verdes Peninsula Unified
  School District 30, 67
Palos Verdes
  Project 83, 106, 112, 114;
  buildings 101, 106, 110,
  116, 119, 122, 124; early
  plans 13, 67, 88, 101, 128;
  history 101, 102, 103;
Palos Verdes Unified School
  District 99
Parklands Controversy 129
Peacocks 89, 90
Pelicans 9
Peninsula Center 96, 98
Peninsula Center Library 97
Peninsula Education
  Foundation 99
Pepper trees 87
Phillips, Harry 51, 83
Phillips Ranch 82, 86
Point Fermin 53, 54, 61, 142
Point Vicente 87, 91
Point Vicente Interpretive
  Center 7, 54, 143
Point Vicente Lighthouse 11
Portuguese
  Bend 28, 87, 89, 141
Portuguese Bend Club 26, 29
Portuguese Bend Lodge 25
Portuguese Point 25, 91
Portuguese whalers 28, 126
Raccoons 69
Radar towers 40
Ramon Sepulveda 52
Rancho de los Palos Verdes 51, 52
Rancho de los Palos Verdes
  Historical Society 25, 82, 91, 118

Rancho Elastico 84, 95
Rancho Palos Verdes 13, 24, 30, 35, 36, 67, 87, 96, 141, 142, 143
Rancho San Pedro 49, 50, 52
RAT Beach 121
RDA 26
Redevelopment Agency 20, 26
Reservoir 70
Rodriguez, Juan Cabrillo 15
Roessler Pool 121
Rolling Hills 68, 82, 83, 85, 86, 102, 141; architectural regulations 84
Rolling Hills Estates 73, 85, 90, 96, 141, 143
Rolling Hills Estates City Hall 83
Royal Palms 49, 54
Sage and sagebrush 33
Sagebrush 33
San Pedro 35, 36, 52, 47, 50, 52, 54, 60, 61, 64, 65, 143
Save Our Coastline 141
Sea lions 16
Sea otters 17
Sea urchins 133
Sepulveda family 49, 52, 66, 71, 82, 107
Sepulveda, Jose Diego 49
Sepulveda, Jose Dolores 50, 51, 71
Sepulveda, Ramon 51
Shipping zones 15
Shoreline Park 35
Skunk 70
Snakes 34
South Coast Botanic Garden 81
South Shores landslide 36
Surfers 125, 131
Swedenborgian Church 22, 23
Tagami, Tamiji 51
Talking Clock 98

Terraces 139
Thomas, Vincent 65
Tide pool creatures 134, 135, 136, 137
Trails 15, 86
Trees 104; coral 8; eucalyptus 86, 116; oak 120; pepper 87
Tumbleweed 28
Tunnels 13, 66
Vancouver, George 11, 47, 49
Vanderlip Estate 88
Vanderlip family 111, 117
Vanderlip, Frank 24, 88, 89, 91, 101, 102, 141
Vanderlip, Narcissa Cox 22, 89
Via Mirlo Gate Lodge 104
Views 8, 37, 40, 60, 87, 100, 106, 125
Villa Francesca 25, 91
Vincent Thomas Bridge 60
Volcanos 25
Walker's Cafe 47
Wallace, Don 93
Wallace Ranch 93
Waste technology 84
Water 24, 26, 71, 72, 73, 83, 86
Wayfarers Chapel 22, 24
Weather 89, 140
Whales: education about 48; Gray whales 7, 10, 11; Killer 19; Pilot 19
Whaling 28
White Point 49, 51, 54, 133
Williamsburg Lane 84
World War I 65, 89
World War II 22, 52, 57, 65, 93, 107, 115, 131
Wright, Lloyd 22
Wrigley, William 15